PRAISE FOR

*JUST CHANGE: HOW TO COLLABORATE
FOR LASTING IMPACT*

"*Tynesia Boyea-Robinson is a rare individual. She has the mind of a scientist, coupled with the heart of a caring philanthropist. The combination yields fresh and powerful insights into the otherwise well-trodden topic of change. What distinguishes her book is that she does not focus her prescriptions on solving problems. Rather, she focuses on ensuring that those problems remain solved. This simple distinction is frequently lost in the social sector, creating the frustrating perception of a merry-go-round with an endless circle of proposals and solutions to address problems that return time and time again.* Just Change *attempts to stop the spinning and achieve lasting impact. Reading it is a ride worth taking.*"

—Michael Powell, president, National Cable & Telecommunications Association

"*Tynesia Boyea-Robinson knows the power of collaboration and collective action necessary to resolve complex challenges and create lasting impact.*"

—Angela Glover Blackwell, founder and president, PolicyLink

"*With wisdom earned in the private and social sectors, Tynesia Boyea-Robinson provides great insights into how systems-level change actually happens—and how you can do more to produce it in your community.*"

—Mario Morino, chairman, Morino Institute

T0272762

JUST CHANGE

HOW TO COLLABORATE
FOR LASTING IMPACT

TYNESIA BOYEA-ROBINSON

Published by Advantage, Charleston, South Carolina.
Member of Advantage Media Group.

ADVANTAGE is a registered trademark, and the Advantage colophon is a trademark of Advantage Media Group, Inc.

Printed in the United States of America.

ISBN: 978-1-59932-776-1
LCCN: 2016959734

Cover design by Katie Biondo.

This publication is designed to provide accurate and authoritative information in regard to the subject matter covered. It is sold with the understanding that the publisher is not engaged in rendering legal, accounting, or other professional services. If legal advice or other expert assistance is required, the services of a competent professional person should be sought.

Advantage Media Group is proud to be a part of the Tree Neutral® program. Tree Neutral offsets the number of trees consumed in the production and printing of this book by taking proactive steps such as planting trees in direct proportion to the number of trees used to print books. To learn more about Tree Neutral, please visit **www.treeneutral.com.**

Advantage Media Group is a publisher of business, self-improvement, and professional development books. We help entrepreneurs, business leaders, and professionals share their Stories, Passion, and Knowledge to help others Learn & Grow. Do you have a manuscript or book idea that you would like us to consider for publishing? Please visit **advantagefamily.com** or call **1.866.775.1696.**

To Grandma Boyea, who taught me to be bold, and to Sydney and Dylan, who remind me why I have to be.

Until one is committed, there is hesitancy, the chance to draw back—concerning all acts of initiative (and creation), there is one elementary truth that ignorance of which kills countless ideas and splendid plans: that the moment one definitely commits oneself, then Providence moves too.

All sorts of things occur to help one that would never otherwise have occurred. A whole stream of events issues from the decision, raising in one's favor all manner of unforeseen incidents and meetings and material assistance, which no one could have dreamed would have come her way.

Whatever you can do, or dream you can do, begin it. Boldness has genius, power, and magic in it.

—Johann Wolfgang von Goethe (1749–1832)

TABLE OF CONTENTS

FOREWORD

We are impatient at Living Cities. We believe the pace of change in this country is too slow, and we will not solve our most intractable problems unless we dramatically alter our behavior to create new opportunities for those who have historically had few.

Yet, with this impatience, Living Cities also recognizes that full-scale dramatic changes take time. We do not think our problems will be solved overnight. In fact, Living Cities has been working on the challenges that plague our cities for twenty-five years now. The institutions that came together to form Living Cities two and a half decades ago aimed to transform communities by creating affordable housing. We have since expanded our scope to focus on fostering economic opportunity by preparing people for those opportunities, connecting them to those opportunities, and creating new opportunities where before there were none.

Living Cities has evolved and grown over these twenty-five years into a member institution of eighteen foundations and financial institutions all committed to these lofty goals. Each of our members has a different motivation for joining our collaborative, but all are committed to creating what we call a "New Urban Practice" that can get those dramatically better results for low-income people we so sorely need across our country.

We work with civic leaders in over a hundred cities to develop and apply the components of this New Urban Practice. These leaders come from all sectors—nonprofit, philanthropic, business, government—and work across multiple issues, such as education, workforce, civic tech, finance, health, financial literacy . . . the list is endless. We are truly cross-sector in our approach because there is no one type of solution to our most pressing problems. Instead, we need to collaborate together to develop solutions for lasting impact.

Tynesia Boyea-Robinson is a true embodiment of Living Cities' values of impatience, collaboration, and audacity. I've known Tynesia for years, and we always seemed to run into each other at opportune moments in our careers. One time we were both at a conference and she ran across a crowded conference room to talk to me about our work at Living Cities. That's when I knew she had to join my team. We have been running together ever since, toward that finish line where the American Dream of equal opportunity is possible for all Americans.

As you will see in this book, Tynesia brings a no-nonsense attitude toward creating lasting impact in communities. She does not overprocess or overcomplicate things when they don't need to be. Many of the concepts and approaches you'll read about in these pages are simple, but deceptively so. The hard work is applying them in your communities, which is why Living Cities is so committed to sharing our lessons learned so you do not have to start from scratch in your work. Think of this book as some of the collective knowledge from Living Cities' twenty-five years of working with leaders like yourself, filtered through Tynesia's own deep experience working in and supporting community change.

Thank you for the work that you do every day to create a New Urban Practice that gets dramatically better results for low-income people. Together, we can create the lasting impact that is so needed in our communities.

Ben Hecht
President and CEO, Living Cities
October 2016

ACKNOWLEDGMENTS

So much of this book is really about the stories of others. Most of these stories were shared freely and publicly by leaders across the country in service of arming others with any information that would make their pursuit of lasting impact more effective. I am so grateful for those leaders we reference throughout the book who sacrifice so much daily for their own communities and are still generous enough to disclose the good, the bad, and the ugly on behalf of communities they may have never seen.

Explicit thanks go to the inaugural leaders of the Integration Initiative: Mary Kay Bailey, Kurt Sommer, Monique Baptiste-Good, Sue Mosey, and Walter Wright. When each of them decided to partner with Living Cities, there was no such thing as collective impact, so they were pioneers for this space. We are so grateful for their support, belief, and partnership. Additionally, there are so many staff members at Living Cities who wrote articles over the course of the past few years. We pulled from many of these articles to share what everyone is learning across our portfolio. It is a rare place where we can learn in public, and it is due to Ben Hecht's vision and Elodie Baquerot and Nadia Owusu's strategy that I had the space to share in the first place.

The rest of the stories shared come from lessons I learned from important people in my life shepherding me during critical inflection points. I have been very fortunate to have parents who raised me and set the foundation of who I am today. My parents were young when I was born, but while times were tough, their youth was not a deficit. My mother is the one who raised me, regardless of whether or not she birthed me. And my father taught us all so much by his example, even if the only thing he often remembers is all the mistakes he made.

I'm grateful to all the mentors I had along the path who saw something in me that I didn't see in myself. The first is Deborah Dean-Nelson, who pushed and supported me to apply for college. She also began to expose me to people who looked like me that were excelling in ways I couldn't imagine. Others include Gerald Chertavian, who gave me trust and space to learn and grow, and my dynamic board duo at Year Up National Capital Region, John King and Bruce Rosenblum, who connected me to resources and support as I figured it out. My "framily," the friends who are so close they might as well be related, have also been wonderful mentors. Marlissa, Monica, and Demetria have been my sisters in arms along the way. (And it helps that my actual sisters, Nychi and Tiki, like them too.)

I learn so much from people who are on my team. The first person who taught me how to be a better leader and manager was Nicolette Berte. She has been my partner in arms ever since. And for this book, my Living Cities team has been a source of fuel and inspiration. Brittany Ramos DeBarros trusted and supported me from day one, Joan Springs protects me, JaNay Queen Nazaire completes me, Tracey Jarmon pushed me, and we have so many new team members

(Hafizah Omar, Ratna Gill, and Shanee Helfer) who have bought into the culture we have built together and jumped in feet first. And without Jeff Raderstrong, this book would not exist. It is because of him that we have kept this project moving forward.

Lastly and most importantly are Keith and my children, Dylan and Sydney. Keith started as my study partner and has evolved into my life partner. He makes me laugh, he takes care of me, he keeps me from taking myself too seriously, and he keeps me present in the moment. And doing this type of work takes sacrifice that most people don't see and it's usually travel away from my family at home. Together, I know that we are raising our two children with care and intentionality. I have so much to be grateful for, and it is because of the role that individuals have played in my life that I'm hopeful of what we can do together to achieve lasting impact.

INTRODUCTION

BRIDGING THE OPPORTUNITY GAP

Growing up, I was often trotted out on stages as an exemplar student. I was a girl who liked math, a person of color who did well in school, and a ham who rarely found a spotlight I didn't love.

As I stood on stage after stage, I'd look out at my parents, and I could see they were swelling with equal parts pride and pain. Often, as I received my accolades, there was a clear implication—I got there *in spite* of my parents and their upbringing (although, actually, this couldn't have been further from the truth). These well-intentioned ceremonies were designed to let "people like me" know what was possible if they just "worked hard enough"—but instead, the ceremonies embarrassed me and set me apart from the people I loved the most.

I came from a jumbled background of opportunity and disadvantage. On my dad's side, my grandparents were from Guyana and

Japan; my mom's family was black from Long Beach, California. My father was the youngest of five children, and his brothers and sisters are traditionally successful—teacher, banker, marketing executive, and engineer. As a teenage father, instead of going to college, my dad joined the military in order to support his young family. Meanwhile, my mom (and my stepmom) came from families where no one had ever gone to college, women often had babies young, and everyone pitched in to raise the children. All these varying approaches to family life shaped who I am today.

My aunts and uncles and my paternal grandmother did a lot of my initial upbringing. They took me to libraries and museums, and I absorbed a sense that the world was full of potential and possibility. My dad's family showed me that there was a big world out there, and I was always looking for new opportunities to learn and grow. In contrast, my mother taught me to find joy and laughter in the midst of sadness and to trust and believe in the good in the world even when you have been hurt by those closest to you. Lastly, my father and stepmom taught me discipline and responsibility. Under their roof, I learned to work hard, admit my mistakes, and channel my gifts toward something bigger than myself. As the firstborn child, niece, and granddaughter, I had access to my first and best opportunity— the commitment, support, and love of a diverse family structure. This support structure provided a strong foundation, and as I grew older, my enthusiasm for achievement attracted more opportunities, including mentors who were eager to help me grow to even higher levels.

Meanwhile, my younger siblings had very different experiences from mine, both good and bad. While I was on those various stages, my little sisters would be sitting in the audience, growing increasingly bored with what they saw as the always-playing *Tynesia Show*.

My introverted middle sister and my artistic youngest sister couldn't help but become annoyed. I don't blame them. Teachers and other adults were always pointing out my achievements to my sisters, hoping they'd be inspired by my example. Instead, they internalized that I was somehow different from them. In reality, they were just as talented and intelligent as I was, but we ended up in very different places.

Why did that happen? I wasn't a better person than my sisters. I wasn't more worthy of attention and praise than they were. Simply because of the accident of birth order, I was exposed to different opportunities at an earlier age. As a result, I had a drive to excel, and my life was fueled by an always-burning passion for achievement.

OVERCOME BARRIERS TO SUCCESS

Later, as I entered the professional world, I was eager to make a difference, and I brought that same passion for achievement to my work. Despite my passion, I kept hitting a brick wall. All my passion and enthusiasm weren't enough to bring about the change I had hoped for. I couldn't escape the same realization I'd had when I was younger: there was a gap between people who had opportunities and those who didn't. For most, these gaps came from a legacy of systemic injustices that kept people from opportunities. I also saw that, as the years go by and people grow older, that gap keeps getting wider.

If you've been fortunate enough to have opportunities, you may not realize what life is like when you don't have those privileges. In a sense, I'd lived on both sides of the opportunity gap, so I could see just how unfair it was to the individuals who don't have the same opportunities that others do. I was constantly being confronted with people who were clearly just as smart, just as hard working, and just as talented as someone else—and yet they didn't have access to opportunity, and so they floundered.

This realization finally came to a head for me when I was leading Year Up National Capital Region, an organization that helps place eighteen- to twenty-four-year-olds in jobs. About 85 percent of the young people we helped were earning close to $40,000 within four months of graduating. I know most people might have said, "Wow, that's an awesome percentage!"—but I couldn't stop thinking about that other 15 percent.

The individuals who made up that 15 percent were intelligent, and they worked hard. But it didn't matter. The systems they'd experienced before we encountered them were broken. Many of these young people were hardworking moms without access to childcare, children who were kicked out of foster homes, or survivors of trauma without mental health services. And while the 85 percent who graduated often had just enough informal support in place to overcome these challenges, the remaining 15 percent were not as fortunate. When those young people who were less fortunate walked through my office door, all I could offer them was a Band-Aid for the broken systems that had failed them.

This isn't acceptable, I thought. I had to find a better way—a way that addressed both the symptoms and the root causes of the problems these young people face every day.

At Year Up, I worked diligently with a host of talented leaders to close what they call the opportunity divide.[1] Those efforts are focused on the systems related to employment and education in service of young adults, and Year Up outcomes are undeniably effective. But bridging these opportunity gaps isn't enough: people face gaps in transportation, homelessness, lack of support, you name it. And as the 15 percent of young adults who did not complete the program get older, the problems they face become more and more challenging.

Today I work at Living Cities. It's a place where I can use my passion to achieve and help narrow the opportunity gaps that so many people of all ages encounter. At Living Cities, we work to build a new type of urban practice that's aimed at dramatically improving the economic well-being of low-income people. We do that by addressing the root causes of the opportunity gaps. Wherever we see a barrier that keeps low-income people from being successful, we invest in removing that barrier, whatever it is.

We remove those barriers through collective problem solving. We have members who are financial institutions as well as large philanthropic organizations. Together, they have the power, the influence, and the resources to invest in things differently, to mobilize leaders differently, and to raise issues differently.

The people who work with me here at Living Cities share a couple of basic characteristics: like me, they are passionate about bringing about change—and they are also restless. They're not satisfied with the way things are, and they're frustrated with the fruitless attempts to bring about change in this country. They're passionate about improving the lives of others, and they're looking for a way to do things differently from what has been done in the past.

Living Cities is a magnet for passionate, restless people like this. It captures their energy, focuses it, points it at specific problems—and then uses that energy to help bring about concrete changes that improve people's lives. It's a wonderful, amazing, powerful thing to observe, but it's not sheer passion alone that makes it happen. Living Cities' work is based on specific, practical ideas and methodologies.

Lack of knowledge and experience can be another sort of opportunity gap that blocks us from doing practical things to pull up the roots of inequality, poverty, and injustice. That's why I've written this book: to give you access to the same information, ideas, and experiences that power Living Cities, so that you too have tools on your journey to bridge the opportunity gaps that hinder people on their path to success. Throughout the book I'll be asking you to consider changing these six things to help bridge whatever opportunity gap you care about:

- how you think about change

- how you create change

- how your organization works

- how you collaborate

- how your collaborative does its work

- how you resource your collaboration

I hope you'll find what we're learning with our partners at Living Cities to be useful and timely. I'm committed to building a country where no parent feels inadequate because of where they started when they began raising their children, where children aren't denied access to opportunities because of the way in which they relate to the world, and where no little girl stands alone on a stage ripped from the very support systems that would sustain her success. I bring to my work at Living Cities the unyielding belief that the intractable problems our country faces are not only solvable but also that the tools exist to achieve them. Together, we can bridge those opportunity gaps.

HOW TO READ THIS BOOK

I wrote this book to share the lessons from my work and the work of Living Cities to help you create lasting impact more easily and readily.

The book is a mixture of stories, lessons, examples, tools, frameworks, and approaches for creating lasting impact. Each chapter and each section can be read separately or together. The components build on each other and overlap in their lessons. Depending on where you are in your journey to create lasting change, you may need to spend more time in some chapters than in others. But it is my hope that you can take what you need from this book and apply it directly to your work.

If you find the lessons in this book useful, I hope you'll share your story of impact with me.

 **_Share Your Story_**

Visit **www.changeforimpact.org** to tell us how you used this book to create lasting impact and Living Cities may highlight your work.

CHAPTER 1

CHANGE HOW YOU THINK ABOUT CHANGE

Bridging opportunity gaps can seem like an impossible task. As far back as high school, however, I have believed that the impossible could be made possible. I learned that when I interned for a summer at NASA.

I was assigned to help build the International Space Station, an enormous project that at first glance seemed like a daunting, if not unattainable, goal—and yet with determination and hard work it was happening right before my eyes. I became convinced that if something as immense and intricate as the Space Station could be built, then, together, human beings could also achieve all sorts of other amazing things.

Our world today faces a host of daunting, complicated, and complex problems: poverty, hunger, lack of educational opportunities, climate change, violence, racism, and sexism. The list is never ending. The struggle to find solutions to all these problems can feel like playing whack-a-mole: just as you knock one down, another one pops up, and then another, and another, and then the same one you knocked down originally is right up there again. It's frustrating, but even worse, it can seem hopeless.

It can make us feel like giving up—but I'm convinced that if human beings can build the International Space Station, then we also have what it takes to tackle the social and environmental dilemmas our world is facing. No matter what shape it takes, we can eliminate opportunity gaps by bringing people together to solve problems. Change truly is possible—but only if we rethink our preconceived notions of what change looks like.

COMPLICATED VS. COMPLEX CHALLENGES

As we work to create change, some of the challenges we face will be complicated—and some will be complex. What's the difference?

Neither one is easy, but a challenge that's complicated can have a set solution. In the case of sending a rocket to the moon, there was no standard solution at first, but NASA found one that could be replicated and easily tweaked for all future moon visits. A complicated solution may have many crazy, moving pieces, but nevertheless, steps can be defined. You might say there's a manual to use, a protocol—a plan that tells you exactly what to do and in what order. The steps may be difficult, but as long as you master them, you can be assured of success. Sending a rocket to the moon is a huge task that requires the coordination of many steps by people with high levels of specialized expertise. When you've successfully done it once, though, the next rocket's requirements will be pretty much the same, meaning that you'll be able to repeat the steps you took the first time around.

A complex problem, on the other hand, cannot have a standardized solution. Each incidence of this sort of problem is one-of-a-kind, involving many interconnected relationships that interact differently and unpredictably in each situation. In complex situations, you might push on something—and discover that you've produced an unexpected change somewhere completely different. Child-rearing is an example of something that's complex: just because you raise one child successfully, there's no guarantee that you can do the same for your next child, even if you tried to duplicate exactly what you did for the older sibling. Each child is unique, and each child's life will be built from countless differing variables, all interrelated in ways over which you have little control.

Sometimes people seem to think that the business world's problems are complicated, while the social sector faces complex challenges that are far more difficult to overcome. That's not actually the case. When the iPad was being developed, for example, it was a complex task. The protocol didn't exist yet, the variables were seemingly infinite, and no steps had been defined for reaching a final product. There was no market for an iPad, so there was no understanding of how the product would be received. And yet the folks at Apple eventually created the iPad and made it a commonplace product. Today, it's a complicated task to continually create new iPads—but not a complex one.

What's true, however, is that the private sector tends to approach challenging tasks with a confidence we often lack in the social sector. When the International Space Station was being built, it required a vast team of people all working together on different pieces to solve problems, discovering the solutions as they went along. They didn't throw up their hands and say, "Sorry, this is just too complex! There's no way we can figure it out." Instead, they pushed forward, finding the answers they needed as they went along. As they did, they captured their results so that they could be repeated.

In the social sector, we can do the same thing. Working together, we can proceed confidently, discovering and defining solutions we can reuse to create lasting impact. It's not easy. When we start, the number of variables is immense—and we don't know which variables are interconnected. But that doesn't mean we can't figure out the connections. We can.

First, however, if we want to achieve a goal as complex as preventing poverty or increasing educational opportunities, then people need to join forces in new ways. Instead of groups fighting in many different directions, we need to come together in a unified vision, working for an agreed-upon outcome. We're going to need to look at the entire system, not just at the individual problems that are merely the symptoms of larger overall problems. And then we must not only find solutions to the problem but also make sure that the solutions don't disappear tomorrow or next year or ten years from now. We want to achieve a lasting impact.

SIMPLE, COMPLICATED, AND COMPLEX PROBLEMS

SIMPLE	COMPLICATED	COMPLEX
Baking a Cake	Sending a Rocket to the Moon	Raising a Child
The recipe is essential.	Rigid protocols or formulas are needed.	Rigid protocols have a limited application or are counter productive.
Recipes are tested to assure easy replication.	Sending one rocket increases the likelihood that the next will also be a success.	Raising one child provides experience but is no guarantee of success with the next.
No particular expertise is required, but experience increases success rate.	High levels of expertise and training in a variety of fields are necessary for success.	Expertise helps but only when balanced with responsiveness to the particular child.
A good recipe produces nearly the same cake every time.	Key elements of each rocket must be identical to succeed.	Every child is unique and must be understood as an individual.
The best recipes give good results every time.	There is a high degree of certainty of outcome.	Uncertainty of outcome remains.
A good recipe notes the quantity and nature of the "parts" needed and specifies the order in which to combine them, but there is room for experimentation.	Success depends on a blueprint that directs both the development of separate parts and specifies the exact relationship in which to assemble them.	Can't separate the parts from the whole; essence exists in the relationship between different people, different experiences, different moments in time.

Source: Westley, F., B. Zimmerman and M. Q. Patton, 2006,
Getting to Maybe: How the World is Changed.

ACHIEVE SYSTEMS CHANGE

Systems change is an approach to creating social change in which change makers take a broad view of complex problems (such as ending poverty or eliminating global warming) to figure out how to solve them. To create systems change, you must look beyond delivering individual programs and think about how to solve fundamental problems in a society. It's a methodology we use at Living Cities to create lasting impact. It requires ongoing feedback that lets everyone know what's working and what's not, allowing us to create a consistent approach that's based on continual improvements to the system.

Systems change is a term that was originally applied to fields such as engineering, biology, and psychology—but the principles work equally well for the social sector. Donella Meadows, a researcher and thought leader whose career spanned decades and disciplines, created and contributed to some of the seminal works on the topic. One of her main contributions to the concept was her insistence that, when tackling a problem, you must shift focus from a problem's symptoms and look instead at the root cause.

Say you have a recurrent cough that just won't go away. You could keep taking a cough suppressant, which would decrease the symptoms—or you could try to determine what was causing the cough. Maybe you need treatment for tuberculosis. Maybe you should stop smoking. Maybe you have an allergy. Until you determine what the actual underlying cause is, you're just playing whack-a-mole with your cough: every time you knock it down, it's going to pop up again.

Systems change requires that you direct your attention to the heart of the issue, because it's not enough to just solve the problem. You must also ensure that the problem *remains* solved. You want to have an impact that endures beyond the life of a program or the people that started the effort. This happens when three things occur:

- You change the way you think about successful impact by using data to define it.

- You shift programs and policies to align with the impact you want to have.

- You align funding streams with your overall goals.

The tools and techniques you'll read about in the rest of the book will help you to do all three of these things to create lasting impact. The rest of this chapter will talk more about the first bullet, to help you think through how to shift your mind-set for how to create change.

DRIVE CHANGE WITH DATA

Before I started working for Living Cities, my company, Reliance Methods, led a Washington, DC, workforce initiative. We had a cross-sector group of leaders—nonprofits, a community college, DC government, and some of the biggest employers in the region—all focused on increasing DC employment. Each institution had a different approach to solving the problem and was accustomed to highlighting all the reasons their program was the most effective. Our collaborative, however, insisted that results for individuals mattered more than results from programs. When it comes down to it, what matters more than attendance in a particular program is that fewer people are unemployed, more people are finding work, and employers are hiring employees to meet their needs.

To know the answer to that question, you need data. Data, whether qualitative or quantitative, validate what works. Data also let you know what doesn't work. Whether you are working within a workforce system or any system, you can't achieve lasting change without knowing those two things.

At Reliance Methods, we started with setting employment goals that were too big for any one organization to achieve on its own during the specified time period. So to achieve that goal, we needed to bring together that cross-sector group of leaders. In our case, the seven organizations ensured that one thousand adults were hired over the three-year grant period. Next, we agreed to share our data with each other not only on what happened when adults were hired but what broke down when adults were *not* hired. Was it program design? Organizational structure and culture? Disconnects with employers? Whatever the reason, we worked diligently to understand what was working, what was not working, and why, by using both quantitative and qualitative data to measure our progress toward our goals.

Data-driven change is the foundation for shifting programs and policies so that they align directly with larger goals for a lasting impact. At Living Cities, we have learned that this means helping the public and private sectors think about change in new ways. It's not enough for organizations to simply collaborate. As the directors of one of our partnering organizations likes to say, "It's a potluck, not poker; it's about what you bring to the table." You have to find out what truly works—and you can't know what that is without data.

One common pitfall when working toward data-driven change is to not know what data to collect to inform decision making. We'll explore that more in chapter 3, but if you can't wait, flip to page 45 to learn more!

 *Case Study*

DC WORKFORCE INITIATIVE

Before I started working at Living Cities, my company, Reliance Methods, led a Washington, DC, workforce initiative. We had a cross-sector group of leaders—nonprofits, a community college, DC government, and some of the biggest employers in the region—all focused on increasing DC employment. Each institution had a different approach to solving the problem and was accustomed to highlighting all the reasons their program was the most effective. But by changing how they thought about change, the leaders were able to see beyond their work and commit to solving a complex problem. The seven organizations involved agreed to a goal of supporting one thousand adults secure jobs over a three-year grant period.

CHALLENGES TO THINKING ABOUT CHANGE DIFFERENTLY

Comfort with Feedback

Even if you start using data and begin thinking about how to change systems, you can still face barriers to thinking about change differently. One of the biggest challenges for working with others to create lasting impact is to become comfortable with ongoing feedback. Each group involved needs to be willing to let go of its control and instead work toward the common focus. This requires transparency; you can't be defensive if the data indicates that something you're doing isn't actually working. Instead, you have to welcome the feedback because it will allow you to change what you're doing so that you can move closer toward the common goal you share and create an impact that lasts.

In the earlier example with the DC Workforce Initiative, it took almost a year for the seven grantees to feel comfortable sharing with each other what *wasn't* working. But once they did, they collectively began doing the unthinkable! They began group pitching to employers to ensure that the best people, regardless of which program they came from, were connected to employment opportunities. They began sharing their trade secrets to make each other better. Together they exceed their collective goal of one thousand employed residents. We'll talk more about how to create an effective feedback culture in chapter 3.

Not Fighting the Right Enemy

Another challenge that can lessen the effectiveness of any group working for change occurs when members feel that the enemy is city government or perhaps a member of the business community. When partners around the table disagree with each other, the enemy can even look like each other.

Instead, as discussed in the book *Tribal Leadership*, all members must keep in mind that the "enemy" is something far larger, and it's one you all share—it's one of the opportunity gaps we talked about earlier, whether that's poverty, insufficient health care, lack of educational opportunities, institutional racism, or unemployment. Whatever the gap is, *that's* your enemy. That's what you're all united in fighting.

Focusing on a High-Profile Figure

When people forget who the real enemy is, they also forget what it takes to create lasting impact. If you don't make a shift to thinking about complex systems change, then you are at risk of focusing too much on the here and now, such as equating the work of one high-profile leader, like a mayor, with the work of a group of people. When that person leaves, for whatever reason, the partnership's drive to have a lasting impact can dissipate or even disappear. The city of Newark, New Jersey, for example, could have let this happen when Mayor Cory Booker transitioned into a new role. Living Cities was working with a cross-sector partnership in Newark called the Strong Health Communities Initiative when Mayor Booker became Senator Booker and left the city. The mayor had been a rock-star politician who brought passion and leadership to the city's cross-sector partnership. His role was to help lead the charge against the common enemy, acting in service of the common goal. Because the cross-sector leaders ensured the initiative didn't just focus on having mayoral support, the initiative was able to survive the mayoral transition.

 **Share Your Story**

What opportunity gaps are you closing? Visit **www.changeforimpact. org** to share your experiences with others and Living Cities may highlight your work.

CHANGE ISN'T EASY

Most of us agree that we want the world to be a better place. But that's never going to happen in any large-scale, global way if we're all working in countless different directions, focused on our own individual efforts.

In order to change the way we think about change, we must be willing as individuals, as organizations, and as institutions to also change in order to create a lasting impact on the entire system. When we're no longer advocates for our own special interests, then we're working together for something far greater. We're actively changing the way we create change.

Looking Forward:
Change How You Think about Change

Questions to consider:

- Are you trying to solve complex problems or merely focusing on complicated ones?

- Are you actively thinking about the different systems that affect your work?

- Are you using data effectively to better understand the work you're doing?

- Are you comfortable receiving and sharing feedback to improve your work?

CHAPTER 2

CHANGE HOW YOU CREATE CHANGE

Twenty-five years ago, Living Cities, then known as the National Community Development Initiative, focused exclusively on affordable housing and community development. In 1991, neighborhoods were declining and our members believed that improving places would help stem the tide of poverty that was sweeping our nation. Our collaborative of philanthropic and financial institutions achieved extraordinary results together—we collectively helped create the affordable housing market; built half a million homes, grocery stores, and schools; and helped shape how local and federal agencies directed billions of dollars of funding. We had a lot to be proud of because we helped transform hundreds of neighborhoods in more than twenty cities across the country.

There was only one problem. We believed that investing in neighborhoods would help reduce poverty. When we looked at the results we achieved not just for places but also for the people who lived in those places, we realized that we had not achieved our ultimate goal. In fact, despite the good work of the last twenty-five years, low-income people remain closed out from many of the opportunities our society offers. People of color, in particular, suffer from lack of opportunity. The median wealth of white households is twenty times that of African American households and eighteen times that of Hispanic households, regardless of education level.[2] The national unemployment rate for white Americans is 4.4 percent compared to 8.1 percent for black Americans and 5.6 percent for Hispanic/Latino Americans.[3] People of color, and black Americans in particular, are much less likely to own their home[4] or access capital to start a successful business.[5]

When we looked at the reality of what had happened in the last twenty-five years, we realized the result we wanted to achieve together hadn't changed. And we realized we needed to change the way we create change to achieve that result.

This chapter will outline six different ways to change how you create change to achieve lasting impact: focusing on bright spots, creating cross-sector partnerships, changing systems through individuals, defining success in terms of people, engaging with the community, and supporting racial equity.

FOCUSING ON BRIGHT SPOTS

Once you change how you think about change to focus on the system instead of the symptoms, it is easy to become overwhelmed. In the case of Living Cities, it wasn't that affordable housing and community development weren't essential elements to eradicating poverty. The challenge was that so were education, health care, and transportation—the list seemed never ending. So where do you start if you want to change how you create change?

The "leverage point" is a concept that's essential to systems change theory, particularly in Donella Meadows' work, where you think about creating change in a place that has a high potential for leverage, such as in city hall or in Washington, DC. But I like to think in terms of "bright spots"—places of potential opportunities for shifting the system in order to create change—a concept explored by the Heath brothers in their book *Switch*. Within every system— whether it's a human body, a city, a business, or an economy—are places where small changes can shift things enough that big changes will result across the system. Donella Meadows refers to these as "points of power," and she compares them to the magical weapons and heroes that turn the tide of evil in myths and legends.[6] Some of these bright spots have more power than others. You may find a change that benefits only a small group of people, but you may find another change that affects more than half of a community. For example, a small change in how a school system teaches its children can have a ripple effect on the whole community.

Unfortunately, people don't always use these points of power correctly. MIT systems analyst and Meadows contemporary Jay Forrester says that people usually intuitively know where a leverage point is, but they push on it in the *wrong* direction. It's as though they mistake the shadow cast by the bright spot for the actual thing. So instead of triggering leverage points for change, they're actually driving their efforts in the wrong direction.[7]

One example of unintended consequences comes from the Latin American Youth Center (LAYC), a well-known and respected nonprofit that serves the Latino community of Washington, DC. I used to work with LAYC when I led Year Up National Capital Region. LAYC had a program targeted at reducing domestic violence among their clients, but when they reviewed their programmatic results, they realized that participants were more likely to believe that domestic violence was an acceptable part of Latino culture. With this shocking revelation that they had been mistaking a shadow for a bright spot, the staff at LAYC quickly changed course and made fundamental changes to their program. These changes focusing on the *real* bright spots led to significant positive impact on participants, such as creating a space where participants felt more comfortable sharing their feelings.[8]

That's also what happened when the teachers and administrators at my elementary school stood one little girl up in front of the rest of the students and said, "Look how much better she is than the rest of you—so why can't you be like her?" Instead of creating the change they wanted, they actually worked against it. What they thought was inspiring actually just highlighted and exacerbated the opportunity gaps that were already in place. They mistook the bright spot's location, and instead of pushing on the spot itself, they slammed themselves against its shadow.

People often make another mistake as well: they sit back waiting for a single hero to come riding in on a horse, carrying a magic weapon that will fix everything—when really, there's no single hero, no single magic bullet. Instead, our world is full of potential heroes and thousands of powerful tools for achieving change. Our job is to identify as many points of power as possible, and then we need to reproduce them. The Heath brothers said in *Switch*, "You need to look for the early glimmers that something is going right. And when you find a bright spot, your mission is to study it and clone it."

The more bright spots you can find and create, the more power you can funnel into creating a lasting impact. When all those bright spots are brought together, they'll cast more light. They'll be able to achieve far greater, wider, and long-lasting change.

The bigger the problem and the more complex it is, the less likely it is that one person, one program, or one organization can achieve change by themselves. Let's say you're an elementary teacher who needs twenty-five new math books in your classroom. For you and your students, this is a big problem—but it's not so big or so complex that, as the teacher, you can't address it by yourself. You can come up with actions to take—like having a fundraiser to buy books and other resources—and accomplish them pretty much on your own. But now let's say the problem that concerns you as a teacher is that about a quarter of your students are absent more than forty days a year. Now your problem is far larger, with deeper roots in the system itself. To address this problem, you'll probably need to partner with a number of individuals, groups, and organizations in order to understand the problem and solve it.

CREATE CROSS-SECTOR PARTNERSHIPS

One of the tools to change how you create change is to build effective cross-sector partnerships. We work to form collaborative groups that include community organizations, businesses, governments—anyone who has a role in achieving the result. You'll learn more about how to build effective cross-sector partnerships in chapter 4.

The challenge with cross-sector partnerships is that as human beings, we all have a tendency to want to form "tribes," people with whom we share common interests that we can express in a common language.[9] (To dive deeper on this topic, check out the book *Tribal Leadership* by Dave Logan, John King, and Halee Fischer-Wright.) It can be a lot of fun to sit around a table with people who share your enthusiasm for a particular cause. You're all on the same wavelength; you agree on what's most important in life. Unfortunately, as passionate as you all may be about your cause, your group may not be the most effective one for achieving a lasting impact on the issues that concern you.

Instead, we achieve the greatest impact when we form partnerships that bring together the groups with the power and authority to generate specific results. Cross-sector partnerships are a key ingredient to creating lasting impact.

Sometimes when people hear the phrase *cross-sector partnerships*, they assume what we're talking about is just a trumped-up face-lift for something lots of folks have been doing for years: collaboration. You've probably experienced old-style collaboration, where people come together, usually at a public event, talk about the work they will do, and then, all too often, go back to doing what they were already going to do before. Or you may have experienced collaborations with other organizations where people work together to develop and deliver a specific program. The problem with this type of collaboration is that it doesn't get at that larger-scale systems change I talked about in chapter 1.

Cross-sector partnerships are much more intentional than old-style collaboration. Together, the members are committed to the philosophy of collective work toward a common agenda. They hold each other accountable. They're willing to leave their egos and their individual interests at the doors, in order to pursue something far bigger than their individual parts.

The behavior of an effective cross-sector partnership is magical to behold, but it is not created by magic. All too often, cross-sector partnerships are focused more on involving representatives from multiple sectors than on what results those representatives agree to achieve together. And one of the most intentional acts of changing how you create change is to invest the time and energy in converting the many "tribes" into one "tribe" focused relentlessly on the results you're working to achieve together. This is not touchy-feely useless work. This is channeling human nature toward outcomes. In the book *Tribal Leadership*, the authors illustrate that the key to organizations achieving uncommon change is to invest in creating a shared identity where the common enemy is not each other but whatever is preventing successful outcomes.

 *Tools*

CHECK-IN QUESTIONS

One tool that helps with creating a shared identity among a cross-sector partnership is using a warm-up or check-in question at a group meeting. These are sometimes called "icebreakers," and the right check-in question can profoundly change the tone of a meeting. They help people on your cross-sector partnership to get to know one another and establish a shared culture.

I've included some check-in questions we've used in the past here. Some are fun, some are more work related, but all help you create a sense of ownership around your cross-sector partnership.[10]

- If you had a spirit animal, what would it be and why?

- What do you think is the biggest obstacle moving the work forward, how do you feel about the group, and what could we do differently to improve our decision-making process?

- If our partnership was a kitchen appliance, what would it be and why?

- What's an interesting story about your name?

Download this tool at http://tools.changeforimpact.org

CHANGE SYSTEMS THROUGH INDIVIDUALS

It's critical for cross-sector partnerships to create a shared identity because, ultimately, each individual member doesn't live with the cross-sector partnership. They go back to their organizations.

When individuals change the way they see the world, they can help their organizations change as well, and when organizations change, entire systems change too. It also works the other way around: when systems change, organizations have room to change, and then individuals are empowered to change. It creates a never-ending cycle. You might think of it as series of concentric circles that look a little like this:

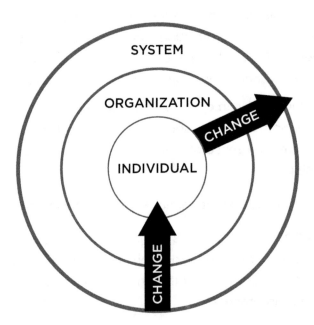

At Living Cities, we've learned that although change moves both ways in this process, it's nearly impossible to start the process at the system level without intentionally focusing on the individual. Instead, you have to get things going at the individual's level and help her change how she thinks about change, as I discussed in chapter 1.

Lasting impact on organizations and systems only occurs when individuals change. What we need to do then is catalyze change within individuals. This is the only way to spark change in the way organizations work internally and with one another.

Preaching at people, however, isn't an effective way to bring about the kind of impact that will endure. In other words, telling people, "You *should* care about issues like poverty and racial inequality," or, "You *ought* to be more tolerant, more generous, or more involved with social issues," will never get you very far.

Daniel Pink's book *Drive* shows how people whose motivation comes from within are far more likely to change. So when you're building your cross-sector partnerships, start with a coalition of individuals who are at least willing to change themselves. If they are willing to change, then they will have the power to change their organization and, together, you will be able to change the systems around you.

DEFINE SUCCESS IN TERMS OF PEOPLE, NOT NEIGHBORHOODS

Even when people are willing to change themselves and their organizations in service of results, it's important to be very clear about what success looks like. Living Cities has been working for years on housing issues. We've helped direct billions of dollars toward neighborhoods and community development—and we've learned that just because you make the neighborhoods better doesn't necessarily mean you make individuals' lives better. A neighborhood might *look* better in terms of income levels, educational opportunities, and so on—but that might be because the people you were working to serve have been driven out of the area.

In addition, even when neighborhoods improve and the people within those neighborhoods are thriving, that does not mean those changes will last or spread to other neighborhoods. To do that, we must also change the overall city policies to sustain "bright spots" beyond individual neighborhoods. Otherwise, we might improve one neighborhood, but our impact won't last—and it won't spread to other neighborhoods—if it's not supported by municipal government policies and support. Remember, you don't want to play whack-a-mole, where you fix one problem only to have it trigger another one somewhere else! You want to get to whatever the root causes are.

SHARE OWNERSHIP WITH THE COMMUNITY

Because success is defined in terms of impact on people, this means that an organization or cross-sector partnership cannot achieve lasting change without authentic involvement and leadership from the community. After all, the community is made up of the people who are experiencing the issues directly, and their perspectives are vital to developing lasting solutions. If they're not engaged, it can feel like what you're offering is patronizing—or even in opposition to their real needs and wants. Imagine if a doctor read on a chart that you had a stomachache and, without consulting you, scheduled you for surgery. As ludicrous as this sounds, similar things are happening in communities across the country by well-meaning leaders.

To create effective engagement, you often must directly confront and combat difference in power dynamics. Cultural differences can make it easier for one group to speak out versus another—but you want to be sure that everyone's voice is heard.

Minneapolis–St. Paul presents a great model for effective community engagement. A team of cross-sector actors, called the Corridors of Opportunity, which Living Cities supported through our multi city collaborative initiative, the Integration Initiative, worked for years on increasing transit opportunities for low-income people so that they could better connect people to job opportunities around the region. They had a great opportunity with the build-out of the Green Line, which connected the downtowns of Minneapolis and St. Paul. They wanted to ensure that city residents were thriving, with affordable housing and access to employment—and they determined that transportation played an essential role in making their goals achievable. It wouldn't matter how many jobs there were if people couldn't get to work, and without work, people wouldn't be able to pay for housing, no matter how affordable it was. So instead of gathering a group of people who merely represented the typical power players in the region, they asked, "Who do we need at the table to make sure that community members have access to the transportation they need? Who has the influence and authority to drive the shared result we're working toward?"

Clearly, they needed municipal government at the table, but they needed to be even more specific than that. The Metropolitan Council is the regional governing authority for Minneapolis–St. Paul's transportation, so naturally the leader of the Metropolitan Council needed to be a part of the group to help create a rail line that would efficiently serve the entire metropolitan area.

The Corridors of Opportunity did a great job bringing together a diverse group of people, all focused on achieving a common goal. In doing this, the group followed the community's cultural practices and customs. They invested in facilitators who were mindful of political dynamics. They made sure that the people with the power and the money didn't drown out the voices of people from the community. They invested trainings so community members could sit on local neighborhood boards and contribute their perspective to planning conversations.

Case Study

CORRIDORS OF OPPORTUNITY

A team of cross-sector actors in Minneapolis–St. Paul, called the Corridors of Opportunity, worked for years on increasing transit opportunities for low-income people so that they could better connect people to job opportunities around the region. They had a great opportunity with the build-out of the Green Line, which connected the downtowns of Minneapolis and St. Paul. They wanted to ensure that city residents were thriving, with affordable housing and access to employment—and they determined that transportation played an essential role in making their goals achievable.

The Corridors of Opportunity did a great job bringing together a diverse group of people, all focused on achieving a common goal. In doing this, the group followed the community's cultural practices and customs. They invested in facilitators who were mindful of political dynamics. They made sure that the people with the power and the money didn't drown out the voices of people from the community. They invested in trainings so community members could sit on local neighborhood boards and contribute their perspective to planning conversations.

Nexus Community Partners, a local community engagement nonprofit, enlisted about a dozen different community groups, including businesses, residents, and nonprofits, as a part of the Green Line planning. They all shared a common agenda, but they put the focus on building a strong and effective relationship with one another and less on the individual projects. They aligned projects with actual needs and, eventually, they were also able to involve the community in advocating for a change in federal policies that would benefit them directly.

Unfortunately, local contexts don't often create an environment where all groups within the community can make their voices heard. In many places, significant work must be done to strengthen relationships between "grasstops" public, nonprofit, and business leaders, and the grassroots low-income residents of the communities in which these organizations operate.

A disconnect between low-income residents and traditional community leaders can be a fundamental problem for collaborating to create lasting impact. While the intention of the grasstops leadership is often well-meaning, community members can serve as a valuable "course-correction check" for potential solutions. Researchers and other practitioners have begun recognizing that community members directly affected by a collaborative's goals are the residents who have important lived experience; they are "context experts." These community members can provide critical insights about the dynamics actually at play in local communities.

In contrast, grasstops leadership and other professionals involved in cross-sector partnerships are the "content experts" who have technical expertise useful for solving specific problems. While these content experts can help identify the structural forces at play and design related solutions, without involving community residents themselves, they won't know whether these solutions are applicable to local context.

My first experience with the difference between content and context expertise was as an engineer working on locomotives in Erie, PA. As a college intern, I was tasked with running tests on our prototype engine. The engineers had worked on the design to withstand heat, using cost-effective materials that met customer specifications (content). But when the prototype engine broke down, the shop floor mechanics had a hard time fixing the problem. This was not because they didn't understand the sophisticated design conjured by the engineers. This was because the design did not take into account the standard wrench size needed to replace the broken parts (context)!

Another example is the city of Albuquerque, NM. They have found a way to bridge this divide between "content" and "context" experts. They work with immigrant entrepreneurs, and Mayor Richard J. Berry has set up "small business deep dives" to make sure he understands the needs of this group of people. These conversations have allowed city hall to know how its actions have prevented immigrant entrepreneurs from succeeding and what it can do to help bridge those opportunity gaps. For example, they are now offering dual-language forms as a way to make it easier for native Spanish speakers to start and run a business.

This work in Albuquerque is a part of another one of our collaborative initiatives, the City Accelerator, which, in partnership with the Citi Foundation, is working to create innovative approaches to community engagement. Atlanta is another member of the City Accelerator, and it is working to manage the gentrification of its Westside neighborhoods. Working with Georgia Tech, Atlanta's city hall is supporting traditionally underrepresented residents to tell their own stories and share their experiences with those who are making the decisions about the Westside neighborhoods.

Your community may not have the same story as any of these cities—but their initiatives illustrate that successful community engagement is possible and necessary, even though it offers ongoing challenges. Communities are complex organisms. They don't come with a step-by-step manual for engagement, and there are no hard-and-fast rules for making community engagement work everywhere, every time.

However, there are some things we know about how to make community engagement successful. Nexus—the organization working in Minneapolis–St. Paul—launched Building the Field of Community Engagement (BTF), a collaborative initiative designed to help others create authentic community engagement. BTF is made up several organizations in the Minneapolis–St. Paul region: a community development organization, an African American cultural health and wellness organization, a Native American community development organization, a Latina/o domestic violence prevention organization, and a multicultural neighborhood organization. They created the "Impacts of Community Engagement" model, which is a useful tool for determining community engagement strategies.[11]

Tools

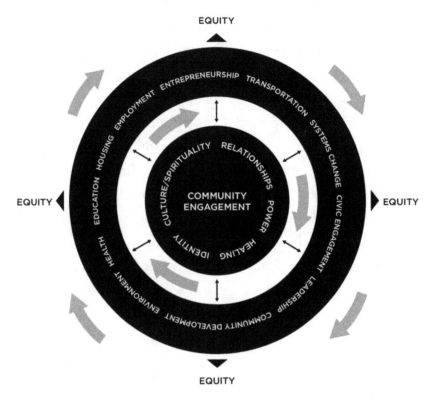

© May 2014 Nexus Community Partners and the Building the Field of Community Engagement partners

Nexus describes the components of the diagram in this way:

- The outer circle outcomes are the tangible, visible goals of the work that community members do together.

- The inner circle outcomes are achieved in the process of doing the work and are foundational elements of a healthy community.

- These assets in the inner circle are the building blocks for positive change in all of the areas of the outer circle and must be attended to or strengthened in a long-term process, during and beyond the process of achieving an outcome in the outer circle. The importance of these elements is often overlooked and communities' work in these areas is often under resourced.

- The wheel as a whole is fluid and dynamic, demonstrating the perpetual interconnectedness of the elements. The model demonstrates the power of community engagement to impact multiple levels and systems and to create sustained change that lasts beyond a project or campaign.[12]

Download this tool at http://tools.changeforimpact.org

CREATE LASTING IMPACT THROUGH EQUITY

On the outside of Nexus' diagram is equity—and that is no accident. Incorporating equity into your work is a fundamental for how you should change the way you create change. Nexus defines equity as the "fair access to resources and opportunities, full participation in the life and well-being of the community, and the self-determination in meeting fundamental needs."[13] Closing opportunity gaps requires a fundamental understanding of how you are creating programs and policies that support and encourage equitable outcomes.

At Living Cities we are explicitly committed to closing opportunity gaps that are the result of racial inequity. As I illustrated at the beginning of this chapter, the biggest gaps in opportunity exist because of race. While many may think we live in a "postracial" society, in fact, systematic and institutional racial discrimination is alive and well. I am not going to spend too much time arguing this case in this book and instead focus on racial gaps as a fundamental requirement for creating lasting impact. That said, explicitly addressing racial inequity as a barrier to lasting impact is new to Living Cities as an organization and me as an individual.

For most of my life I was not comfortable talking about how race affected me. But I didn't shy away from sharing my "melting pot" heritage. My paternal grandparents are Japanese and Guyanese, and my maternal grandparents are black American. I am the walking embodiment of the promise of America as a land of opportunity. In my upbringing I can sing the song of immigrants seeking and finding opportunity. I can spread the harmony of hard workers and bootstraps. Those narratives are easy to hear, and I also learned at an early age that you get more done when people in power listen to you. And I vowed that I would learn to change things from the inside out.

I've always felt rewarded when people in power know that I will prioritize their comfort. And for the most part, very few people in power are comfortable addressing issues related to race. And since I care deeply about results and impact, I worked hard to be nonthreatening. So when I worked in the for-profit world, I tried to hide in plain sight. I steered away from any projects related to diversity. I wanted people to not see my race. I wanted them to see my intellect and my hard work. And while I understand internalized oppression now, in the past I didn't realize that the fact that I believed that being a black woman somehow meant I wasn't intelligent and hard working was a crime in and of itself. And even now, I don't know if I made the right decisions. But what I do know is that every time I got promoted, it made those in power comfortable that our company didn't have a "diversity problem."

You may think working in nonprofits makes it easier to address issues related to race and opportunity. In many ways, it is actually harder. When I fundraised for my social enterprise, very few donors wanted to hear about structural inequities. Instead, their donation made them comfortable and gave them proof that they are good, nonracist people.

You may think working in philanthropy would make it easier to address issues related to race. But I have found it even harder still. On the one hand, there are many more discussions about inequity. On the other hand, there is very little acknowledgment or action about the role philanthropy plays in perpetuating those inequities. And so talking about race makes us comfortable that we're doing something about race.

And so maybe it's time for us all to be uncomfortable. Because all of us will have to change ourselves if we want to change the systems that consistently result in disparities. And each one of us has a role to play if we want this country to truly be a land of opportunity. If you want to learn more about the importance of a focus on equity, I encourage you to check out the resources of PolicyLink, as well as the Government Alliance on Race and Equity (GARE).

 Share Your Story

How is your partnership closing the gaps of racial inequity? Visit **www.changeforimpact.org** to share your story and Living Cities may highlight your work.

COMMUNITY CHANGE AS COLLECTIVE IMPACT

So far I've outlined six different ways to change the way you create change: focusing on bright spots, creating cross-sector partnerships, changing systems through individuals, defining success in terms of people, engaging with the community, and supporting racial equity. This may seem like a lot (it is!), but, gratefully, many of these concepts are captured in a framework that's now referred to as *collective impact.*

A group of consultants at Foundation Strategy Group (FSG) first gave collective impact its name in 2011 by laying out five different components: common agenda, shared measurement, mutually reinforcing activities, continuous communication, and a strong backbone organization.[14] Implementing these five components as a part of your cross-sector collaboration can help you change the way you create change in many of the ways outlined in this chapter.

Even though collective impact got its name in 2011, it's actually been around for decades. Living Cities was first introduced to the concept through our work with the StrivePartnership in Cincinnati.

In 2006, community leaders in Cincinnati and northern Kentucky gathered together to figure out the best way to prepare low-income kids for college. At one point in the meeting, the county coroner stood up and said, "As long as we remain program rich and system poor, we will not get more kids into college. And what's more, I'm going to continue to see dead kids on my table."[15] This declaration led leaders to a conversation about how they could change the way they created change. This conversation led to the creation of the StrivePartnership, which engaged cross-sector community leaders to commit to improving student outcomes. More than three hundred leaders of local organizations—including corporations, city government, schools, universities and community colleges, and nonprofit groups—abandoned their individual agendas and agreed to unify their efforts on a single focus. They realized that the old approach of each tackling separate problems—such as healthier school lunches, better after-school programs, or decreasing the number of high-school dropouts—wasn't significantly improving student outcomes. They realized that real change wouldn't happen unless all parts of the educational system improved at the same time. Instead, they decided to coordinate improvements at every stage of a young person's education, from "cradle to career."

To accomplish this, they didn't create new educational programs or try to raise more money. Instead, they focused the entire educational community on a single set of goals, measured in the same way—and as a result, during Strive's first five years of existence, forty of the fifty-three educational outcomes it measured had improved. There was a 9 percent rise in kindergarten readiness, an 11 percent increase in high school graduation, and a 10 percent increase in college enrollment.

Living Cities worked with the StrivePartnership to figure out what elements of their approach could be replicated to help others around the country achieve similar results. Today, the StrivePartnership has grown into StriveTogether, and it has spread beyond the Cincinnati region to include more than sixty communities. Not only is StriveTogether improving the nation's educational system, but it has also inspired the entire collective impact movement.

FSG studied Strive's results in the educational world, as well as the results of a couple of other examples of this type of community change work, and produced the first article on collective impact in 2011. Since then, the popularity of collective impact as a framework for community change has exploded. FSG and the Aspen Forum for Community Solutions established the Collective Impact Forum, whose mission is to help foundations, businesses, nonprofits, and governments around the world accelerate progress. The Collective Impact Forum is also constantly learning from practitioners about what works and what doesn't in collective impact and refining the framework. Today, more than fifteen thousand people have joined the forum, all working together to create changes that will have a lasting impact.

Examples of collective impact are common outside the social sector as well. For instance, in the scientific world, scientists recently made an important discovery that gravitational waves actually do exist—and they were able to achieve this because of large-scale cross-sector collaboration. What started out as collaboration between the National Science Foundation, Caltech, and MIT, now has more than a thousand contributors from more than eighty scientific institutions.[16]

COLLABORATION		COLLECTIVE IMPACT
Convene around Programs/Initiatives	→	Work Together to Move Outcomes
Prove	→	Improve
Addition to What You Do	→	Is What You Do
Advocate for Ideas	→	Advocate for What Works

The folks at StriveTogether have a great visual of the difference between collaboration (i.e., coordinated impact) and collective impact.

ENDLESS CHANGE?

Across all the communities we've highlighted, the efforts of successful impact triggered other changes. For example, in Minneapolis–St. Paul, once the Green Line launched a few years ago, the Corridors of Opportunity recognized that a huge dent had been made in increasing needed transit infrastructure. And they also embedded policies within the Metropolitan Council that ensured future transit projects would follow similar processes to ensure that residents benefit from new transit lines and stops. So they have rebuilt their cross-sector partnership to focus on creating new jobs for the low-income people that now have access to transit.

And this isn't the end—not in Albuquerque, Cincinnati, or in Minneapolis–St. Paul. All cities have many more changes to undergo because change is never a one-time, one-place thing. It ripples outward in ever-increasing circles of impact. It touches individuals' lives, but it also triggers a cascade of changes—even in the way our own organizations function.

Looking Forward:
Change How You Create Change

Questions to consider:

- Are you looking at the right "leverage points" in your work?

- Are you a part of a cross-sector partnership, or can you build one?

- How can you change individual mind-sets to change systematic structures?

- Have you defined your success in terms of people?

- Do community members have shared ownership with your work?

- Have you considered issues of equity, particularly racial equity, in your work?

CHAPTER 3

CHANGE HOW YOUR ORGANIZATION WORKS

When I made my first leap into the social sector scene from my career in the private sector, I succeeded admirably in one thing: irritating most of the people I worked with. I was used to asking questions in terms of "accountability," "corrective action," and "metrics." When I didn't hear any answers coming back at me in the same language, I assumed (and we all know what happens when you do that) that it just wasn't there. At that point, I started to come across as patronizing. I learned the hard way that the private, public, and social sectors use different terminology for the same concepts. That doesn't mean we don't want the same things; we just approach them in different ways.

During my work in youth development, I heard the term "feedback culture" a lot—and I realized it meant exactly the same thing I'd been talking about when I referenced things like "continuous improvement" or being accountable to specific metrics. Each young person we worked with had to sign a contract committing themselves to professional behavior (accountability). At the end of each week, what they did or did not do well was read in front of their peers by category (metrics). The young person then had the opportunity to change behavior based on this feedback (corrective action). For the young people I had the privilege of serving, the end result was a career pathway to make a better life for them and their families.

As adults, we often resist this kind of feedback. Say your employer decided to use a specific set of criteria to evaluate your work weekly and then expected you to change your behavior based on this feedback. Would you welcome the opportunity to do your job more effectively—or would you feel anxious and defensive?

At Living Cities, however, we believe that lasting impact occurs when we are open to constructive feedback. Data-based feedback allows a cross-sector partnership to define and collectively agree to shared results initiated by behavior changes.

These behaviors are based on a continuous loop of measures and outcomes that let the members of the partnership know whether they're on the path that will successfully take them to their shared goal. Thus, organizations must change how they work internally. Sometimes they may have to sacrifice funding opportunities or decide not to develop a new program because it does not link up to achieving the overall goals of the partnership.

Because this kind of organizational change has so many moving pieces, making it happen can be messy and confusing. You can't just throw things randomly into the mix. Instead, you must carefully implement an entire utility belt's worth of tools. You must be intentional about changing how your organization works.

There are two approaches to changing how your organization works. You can't do one without the other. The first step is to use the intrinsic motivation of the people who work in your organization. The second is to develop a data-driven feedback loop to direct the work of your organization and your partners to create lasting change.

TAP INTO INTRINSIC MOTIVATION TO ACHIEVE RESULTS

A few years ago, AARP asked a group of lawyers if they'd be willing to assist retirees with limited incomes by reducing their legal fees to $30 an hour. The lawyers said no. Then AARP came back with a counteroffer: Would the lawyers offer their services for free to needy retirees? This time, the majority of the group said yes![17]

Psychologists interpret this counterintuitive action on the part of the lawyers as having to do with intrinsic versus extrinsic motivation. Monetary payment is a form of extrinsic motivation—and what the lawyers were being offered just wasn't enough to motivate them. When the lawyers were asked to provide free services, however, AARP accessed a deeper level of motivation. This time, instead of saying to themselves, "My services are worth a lot more than $30 an hour," the lawyers were in effect telling themselves and the world, "I'm the sort of person who wants to help people in need." They were intrinsically motivated to help the retirees.

Stereotypically, people in the social sector are considered more likely to be intrinsically motivated, while people in the private sectors are often thought to be extrinsically motivated by financial factors. What we've learned is that if we can marry the results-driven relentlessness of the private sector with the boundless intrinsic motivation of the social sector, we create a culture that taps into both—and becomes an engine that can drive lasting impact.

HARNESS INTRINSIC MOTIVATION THROUGH MAC

The engine of intrinsic motivation is powerful, if you can harness it correctly. There are many ways to manage and direct people based on their personal motivations, but I've developed a model that I call "MAC." (Another resource to check out is Daniel Pink's *Drive*, mentioned earlier.) I've used the MAC model as a way to organize my team to make sure that we're getting the results we need to get while being personally fulfilled.

The components of MAC are:

- **Model Behavior**: What does it look like to consistently demonstrate the change we seek in the world? We must apply the spirit of lasting impact into our day-to-day work, exemplifying the actions and practices we look to see from partners.

- **Align Resources**: How do we move beyond the resources we control individually to the resources we share collectively to achieve change? Going above and beyond collaboration means applying a systems-level approach to system problems, pooling collective resources (information, financial, political, human capital), and using the connections to solve the problems.

- **Catalyze Change**: How can we harness the power of what *is* working in communities to encourage others to do the same? We do this by influencing policy, practices, and cultures so that there can be shifts at the individual, organizational, and system-wide levels.

We've found MAC to be a great tool. As we implemented it, we created MACtivities, the individual activities we've found to operationalize the principles of modeling behavior, aligning resources, and catalyzing change. They include culture and infrastructure, critical friendships, content building, convening, network weaving, and storytelling and tool building.

 *Tools*

MACtivities

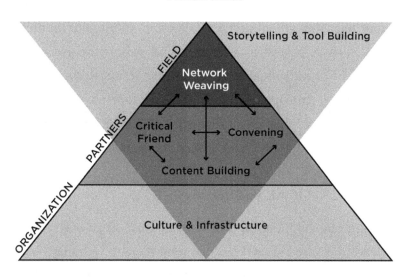

The MAC framework, designed in partnership with Nicolette Berte of Amito Consulting.

Download this tool at http://tools.changeforimpact.org

INVEST IN CULTURE AND INFRASTRUCTURE

When I was in business school, we had a class devoted to leadership. Frankly, most of us, including me, brushed it off as the touchy-feely "soft" class. We would also have the CEOs of the case studies we were reading come to our class. And every time they were asked, "What's one thing you wish you would have done differently?" They would say, "Pay more attention in this leadership class." Time and again, we read stories of organizations failing because of not being intentional about investing in the growth and development of their own people. Similarly, when these leaders made a commitment investing in their culture and values, they achieved amazing returns.

It is even more important to invest in culture and infrastructure when working toward social change. Without an overall culture and an infrastructure to support an organization or team, lasting impact is impossible. Strengthening this area requires investment in internal systems, such as payroll or accounting, as well as the growth and development of individual members of the group, through professional development opportunities. These are not wasted overhead. These are the multiplier effects that will unleash the limitless passion of leaders toward the change we seek in the world!

CREATE CRITICAL FRIENDSHIPS

When I'm out shopping for a new dress, I like to go with my best girlfriends, because I know I can count on them to be honest. When I ask them, "How do I look in this?" I know that if they tell me, "Girl, you look *good*," I really do look good. And if they wrinkle up their noses and say, "Try on another dress," I respect their opinions. I trust them to have my best interests at heart. They're not going to stroke my ego, and they're also not going to criticize me just to be mean. They sincerely want to make sure I buy the most flattering dress out there.

When it comes to partners that are working together toward shared goals, having that same level of trust and honesty is essential. We've found that developing those kinds of relationships is an essential MACtivity that needs to be in place between members of a partnership. It relies on a solid relationship between individuals, one that is strong enough to allow them to push each other in constructive and productive ways to ensure they are achieving their results.

Our commitment to MAC means that we expect ourselves to model the behaviors we ask of other groups (in other words, we want to practice what we preach)—and that includes being open to critical friendships. We support a set of leaders across the country working with cross-sector partnerships through our Integration Initiative. At one point in the history of the initiative, things were a little rocky between us and those leaders. We decided to set up a feedback session to hear their concerns.

They gave us an entire list of all the specific places where they saw us falling short. I can't pretend that it was a whole lot of fun hearing what they had to say—but we're truly committed to the process of aligning our actions with the feedback we receive. We walked away from the meeting determined to show them that we would take action based on the feedback they'd given us.

Over the next few months, we went through the list of challenges and checked off their items one by one. We told them, "Okay, we'll fix this . . . and we'll fix that . . . and that." On a few items, though, we had to say, "We can't fix this—and let us tell you why." Once or twice we said, "We disagree with you about this point," and then we explained our reasons. And on at least one item, we said, "We're not quite sure how to achieve this. Would you partner with us on it? Could you help us fix it?"

Ultimately, what I loved most about this experience wasn't that it helped Living Cities as an organization improve how we function (although it did). What I found most exciting was the way it helped to build a strong relationship of honesty and trust between us and the leaders we support.

BUILD UNDERSTANDING THROUGH CONTENT

For partners to be good critical friends to each other, they need to understand when they need to bring in the skills and expertise in the related content areas of their work. Sometimes a challenge is about what you do, and other times it's about how you do it. When the challenge is the "what," content expertise is critical. The type of content expertise that's required will be different for different groups. It could be an understanding of cutting-edge educational programs, it might be facilitation competencies, or it could be policy analysis. It all depends on what's needed to achieve the results of your cross-sector partnership.

Content building is not just traditional research and subject matter experts. One huge gap in achieving lasting impact is the chasm between research and practice. According to Dr. Andrew Balas, it takes seventeen years, on average, for only 14 percent of research to translate into practice.[18] Oftentimes, this is because the experts are rewarded for being backward-looking and reflecting on why something occurred over time. This isn't responsive to what many communities are facing. At times, it is as straightforward as "something is working in another place that others just don't know." But most times, it is "research has proven something so we know *that* it's important but we don't know *how* to actually do it."

CONVENE COHORTS OF PEERS

Throughout all of our collaborative initiatives, Living Cities has found that regularly bringing together partners can help dramatically accelerate the work to achieve lasting impact. We bring together the people involved in the Integration Initiative at least once a year for a two-day, in-person "Learning Community." By convening people regularly—whether that's people within the same geographical area or from around the country—individuals can share their own perspectives and the lessons they've learned. This transfer of ideas means that initiatives don't have to constantly start from scratch; instead, they can build from the collective knowledge of their peers. Convening allows each participant group to leapfrog off the efforts of all the others because each partner learns from the other. This leapfrogging then expands the scope for lasting impact.

One of the best ways to ensure that convenings actually result in leapfrogging is to keep the outcomes you're working to achieve at the center of your work. For example, multiple sites in the Integration Initiative are focusing on increasing employment. Over the past two years, one of the most moving and challenging issues with employment has been in New Orleans. Our partners there, the Network for Economic Opportunity, were dealing with the extreme challenge that 52 percent of African American men are unemployed in New Orleans. That's thousands of uncles, brothers, fathers, and sons that have so many barriers to employment.

Despite all these challenges, the Network for Economic Opportunity is making real progress. In fact, after two years of partnerships with Living Cities, unemployment among African American men is now down to 44%. There is still a long way to go, yet people who have consistently convened with those leading the New Orleans work are inspired and motivated by their example. In turn, New Orleans feels an even greater sense of accountability now that others are looking to them for guidance. It creates a virtuous cycle where each community is learning from and with each other in service of outcomes with healthy competition on who can combat their biggest enemy—unemployment.

STORYTELLING AND TOOL BUILDING

Storytelling is a MACtivity I love because I *love* to tell stories! I know they have great power. They shape us, inform us, inspire us, and spur us to action. Storytelling breaks down the individual silos that can limit our efforts and allows us to instead see resources and possibilities as they exist throughout the entire collective partnership. Stories give us fresh perspectives; they can make us say, "Oh my gosh, I never looked at it like *that*," or, "Now that I see things from *that* perspective, we're no longer stuck, unable to move forward toward our goal," or, "You've given us a new idea, you've inspired us with fresh passion, you've helped us see a way forward." Or even simply, "If *they* can do it, so can we."

One of the best historical examples of this is *Uncle Tom's Cabin*. When Abraham Lincoln was introduced to the book's author, Harriet Beecher Stowe, he reportedly said, "So you're the little woman who wrote the book that made this great war." Lincoln may have been flattering the author, but historians agree that *Uncle Tom's Cabin* had a tremendous influence on American culture, sparking antislavery passions. Internationally, *Uncle Tom* was the best-selling novel of the nineteenth century, and its influence across the Atlantic helped persuade the British not to side with the South; if they had, the South might have triumphed.

Stories told on television also have power to change individuals' attitudes (which, in turn, leads to change at the organizational and then system levels). Over the last two decades, for example, American attitudes toward homosexuality became rapidly more tolerant—and social scientists have given some of the credit to the sitcom *Will and Grace*.[19] Over almost fifteen years in prime time and syndication, tens of millions of Americans came to know and like Will and his friend Jack. The show opened the minds of many Americans to the fact that gay people are no different than straight people.

Within collaborative initiatives, storytelling allows members to learn from each other. Our success stories let one group see what works for others, so that they may be able to duplicate it, while our failures can be cautionary tales that can help others reconsider their actions. The stories from an initiative in San Francisco can inspire Minneapolis–St. Paul to take action, or New Orleans might gain an important strategy from a story told by King County, Washington. The goals may not be the same—one initiative could be working for health improvements, while the other is targeting community development—and yet common strategies may be able to be employed.

Storytelling breaks down the individual silos that can limit our efforts and allows us to instead see resources and possibilities as they exist throughout the entire collective partnership. Today, there are platforms and technologies that support us in cocreating stories so that they reflect multiple perspectives, voices, and experiences. This means that we can tell stories that are nuanced, complex, and provocative. We can offer multiple ways of looking at an issue. We can invite others to contribute in order to expand our knowledge base. For example, a recent report that Living Cities put out about what it will take to close the racial gaps in income and wealth in America invited folks from our member institutions and partner organizations to add their perspective. The result was a much richer picture of the issue and the opportunities to address it than we would have been able to paint on our own.

Sharing our stories also means that we can celebrate the smaller wins as we work toward the larger, more distant goal. We can bring people along on the journey over time. What's more, they allow us to build tools that can be adapted and used again and again, in a variety of settings. If you can't tell your story effectively, no one will be able to understand the work you are doing, no one can benefit from your learning, and no one will be able to engage fully with you as a partner. Building tools and resources to help you and your partners do your work better is an important component of effective storytelling—telling your story helps you share your lessons learned; tools and resources help others implement those lessons. For example, our partners at StriveTogether have created several case studies on their network members to help others learn from different communities around the country. They have also supplemented these case studies with toolkits to help apply lessons learned.[20] For Living Cities, this book is an opportunity for us to share many of the tools and resources we've created—in fact, this book itself is a big part of our current storytelling strategy!

NETWORK WEAVING

You also need to be looking outside of your cross-sector partnership to what's happening beyond your immediate area of work. There could be opportunities for learning outside your geographical scope—or something might be happening in your own backyard that has a connection to your work you never considered before. If you aren't out there weaving networks, then you'll never know what you're missing!

Once change gets rolling through the medium of collective action, there's truly no limit to how far it will reach. A small change here catalyzes a large change over there. The changes in one individual can spark off changes in another—and together they can work to change an entire organization. That organization can then impact another one that's working alongside it, and the change can spread wider and wider, creating a network of lasting impact.

This may seem like too much additional work when you think about just how difficult it to just get the work done in front of you. But the concept of exposing yourself to outside views is important for leveraging the full potential of your work. I think about my experience in business school, where each person in my section was hand selected with different professional and personal backgrounds. Each class I attended opened my eyes to a different world view, which gave me different ways to see the same problems.

CATALYZE CHANGE THROUGH MAC

The City of Detroit's work as a part of Living Cities' Integration Initiative illustrates how using the principles of MAC can make a difference in the lives of low-income residents. Detroit was focusing on population density and growth within the city as the central factor contributing to job growth and wage increases. The members of the initiative kept asking, "Why can't we get people to move back to Detroit?" The city looked like a ghost town in many areas, with broken-down properties on every street. No one wanted to move there, because, quite frankly, it was a scary place. The problem seemed overwhelming. The city lacked money, and there were thousands and thousands of empty properties. What could they possibly do that would make any difference?

They decided that instead of focusing on what they *didn't* have, they aligned the resources that *were* available—like technology—with the problem in order to act as a multiplier for the resources they *did* have. So they started "texting the blight"—"blexting." They had residents text information about blight around their neighborhoods to help the city understand where areas of need were.

Ultimately, in the middle of a bankrupt municipal administration, texting the blight was able to get every single property catalogued. Doing this tapped into the intrinsic motivation of Detroit's residents, even though it wasn't necessarily the same for everyone. The motivation for some people was, "I really care about my city." Other people's motivation was safety: "I'm freaking scared to walk down this street." Still other people were angry: "The city needs to get their crap together and fix this issue."

 *Case Study*

CITY OF DETROIT

The City of Detroit was focusing on population density and growth within the city as the central factor contributing to job growth and wage increases. The members of the initiative kept asking, "Why can't we get people to move back to Detroit?" The city looked like a ghost town in many areas, with broken-down properties on every street. No one wanted to move there, because, quite frankly, it was a scary place. The problem seemed overwhelming. The city lacked money, and there were thousands and thousands of empty properties. What could they possibly do that would make any difference?

They decided that instead of focusing on what they *didn't* have, they aligned the resources that *were* available—like technology—with the problem in order to act as a multiplier for the resources they *did* have. So they started "texting the blight"— "blexting." They had residents text information about blight around their neighborhoods to help the city understand where areas of need were. Ultimately, in the middle of a bankrupt municipal administration, texting the blight was able to get every single property catalogued.

Regardless of their motivation, together they were able to weave a network of individuals and groups who had a powerful story to tell. The Detroit partnership not only changed the way it worked internally, it also changed the way in which it worked with other organizations and groups within the city.

 ## *Share Your Story*

The elements of MAC and MACtivities have worked well for our attempts to create lasting impact. They are basic concepts, but the combination of each element has helped accelerate our work internally and in communities around the country. If you think they'd be useful, adapt them from your own work. If they help you create lasting impact, share them with us at **www.changeforimpact.org** so we can share your lessons with others. We hope they will help you change the way you collaborate!

CREATE A FEEDBACK CULTURE

A feedback culture is what gives the intrinsic motivation engine its fuel. To achieve a lasting impact on the world, we need to create organizations that are comfortable with a feedback culture. As leaders, we all need the courage to share what's going well and what's not going well—and why—in order to improve continuously. This requires building trust that everyone in the group is coming from a place of caring rather than criticism. What's important is that everyone is on track toward the common goal. Successfully reaching the end result is well worth any temporary discomfort.

The most important part of a feedback culture is whether feedback will allow individuals to better understand what needs to be done to reach a goal—and then change accordingly. As Jeff Edmondson, founder of StriveTogether, and his team often say, "The best data doesn't help you prove, it helps you *improve*."

A feedback culture is made up of various different "feedback loops." A feedback loop creates an automatic process that continually provides an organization or a cross-sector partnership with the information it needs to keep on track. It's not the same as an "information technology system," which could be collecting the wrong sort of information altogether. A feedback loop requires the collection of data, such as number of people served in a week, but it has to be the right kind of data. I've noticed that, many times, when people start thinking about data, they go on a mad spree trying to collect *every* possible piece of information they can: the number of blades of grass in a field, the speed of the wind during April, the rainfall percentages over the course of the summer. Unless that data helps you in some way to determine whether you're closer to your goals, then you don't need it!

The best feedback loops are processes that are elegant and iterative. They let you know the validity of your choices as quickly as possible, like the blinking speedometer signs in school zones, where the flashing numbers inform you whether you should speed up or slow down. Of course, your choice to do so is still ultimately your own, and it's the same with any organization's feedback loop. You need your feedback firmly integrated with your commitment to your results.

One of the methods I like to use to help build a feedback culture is called STAR: situation, task, action, result. Here are the different components:

- Situation/Task: What was the problem, opportunity, challenge, or task that you want to give feedback on?

- Action: What was said or done to handle the situation or task?

- Result: What was the impact of the person's efforts and how did that influence the result?

You give feedback to someone on your team by describing the situation and the task and then talk about the action the feedback receiver did and the result of that action. As you define and discuss each element, it creates a framework where people can feel more comfortable sharing both positive and constructive feedback. Receiving this kind of feedback doesn't mean you're a bad person or that one group is better than another. STAR allows you to simply talk through how choices affect results. It allows you to see what you need to continue doing and what you need to change.

What we discover when we have established a feedback culture is that the root cause of our problems could be something as simple as, "You didn't send us an email on time." The delay in the message being received caused a backlog of work, which interfered with a specific short-term goal being met. The person who failed to send the email may feel defensive and offer excuses: "My workload is so heavy that there's no way I can stay on top of my email," or, "I didn't send that email until later because I had a personal emergency." In a feedback culture, there's no need to feel defensive. No one is saying that the person who failed to send the email is a bad person. Instead, the group can together figure out ways to prevent the same thing from happening again.

Whether the feedback is positive or constructive, the most important follow-up is to ask why continuously. Why was everyone delighted by our last event? Why was that email not sent on time? Why did we attract more investment in the second quarter versus the first? Why is this so much more important than that? When you truly understand and are committed to the why, it helps increase the likelihood that you will increase what's working and reduce what isn't.

This sort of analysis can't be done only once a year or even once a quarter. The "loop" factor is essential. Data must be delivered in a continual cycle that endlessly provides relevant information. And this data should be both qualitative—"our clients feel unappreciated when we don't communicate"—and quantitative—"our clients have improved their healthy behavior by 15 percent." The most important benchmark is not whether the data is quantitative or qualitative. The most important benchmark is whether the data collected helps you to understand the "why" behind your results and allows you to make adjustments accordingly to help you get to the result you're trying to achieve.

GROW CULTURE USING DATA-DRIVEN FEEDBACK LOOPS

Reading over the MACtivities and learning about feedback culture, I'm sure you already have a lot of ideas about how you can rework your organization to better tap into the intrinsic motivation of your people. But creating a feedback culture and leveraging MAC is only the first step. You also need to use data to ground your feedback loops in the day-to-day work.

Adding an element of continuous data collection and sharing to your feedback loop creates what we call a "data-driven feedback loop." You can think about the data-driven feedback loop as a way to operationalize the concepts of feedback culture and feedback loops. In the data-driven feedback loops, there are four different components: key drivers, three-to-six- and six-to-ten-year outcomes, and a shared result. A data-driven feedback loop ensures that strategies are both aligned and on track with the overall goals of the initiative.

 *Tools*

DATA-DRIVEN FEEDBACK LOOP

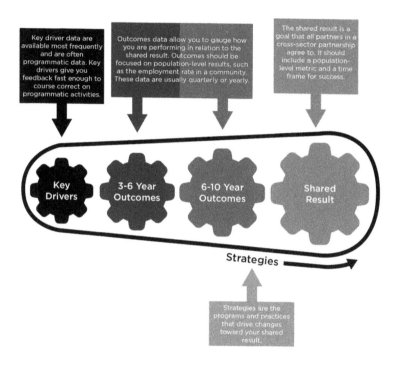

Key driver data are available most frequently and are often programmatic data. Key drivers give you feedback fast enough to course correct on programmatic activities.

Outcomes data allow you to gauge how you are performing in relation to the shared result. Outcomes should be focused on population-level results, such as the employment rate in a community. These data are usually quarterly or yearly.

The shared result is a goal that all partners in a cross-sector partnership agree to. It should include a population-level metric and a time frame for success.

Key Drivers — 3-6 Year Outcomes — 6-10 Year Outcomes — Shared Result

Strategies

Strategies are the programs and practices that drive changes toward your shared result.

Download this tool at http://tools.changeforimpact.org

Your organization can create its own data-driven feedback loop, but that conversation should include your cross-sector partners to make sure your work is aligned. If you do not all agree on a shared data-driven feedback loop, it will be much more difficult to tackle complex problems to create lasting impact. Chapter 4 will go into more detail on how to set up a cross-sector partnership to facilitate these kinds of conversations.

COLLECT THE RIGHT DATA FOR
YOUR FEEDBACK LOOP

Recently, when I was speaking at an environmental conference, we discussed an initiative that had the goal of reducing carbon dioxide emissions in Washington, DC, by 25 percent in five years. I asked the attendees, "What are you doing to drive this change?"

The answers came fast and furious:

"Plant trees!"

"Engage employers to change their polluting behaviors."

"Burn down power plants." (That last one was a little alarming but every room has a wild revolutionary.)

Then I asked them how they would collect data on the initiative. Again, the room was full of answers:

"Report the number of trees planted."

"Have a website where employers who agree to change their polluting behaviors will sign up so that their numbers will be recorded."

"Keep a tally of burned-down power plants." (There was that same revolutionary again.)

Everyone understood the concept of collecting data. But then I asked, "So how will you know if the carbon dioxide emissions are actually reduced? How will you determine how much closer your efforts are getting you to your 25 percent reduction in emissions?"

Pretty much everyone scratched their heads and looked puzzled. They didn't know how to determine the information that was most essential to indicating their success or failure.

It's a common mistake. Organizations can easily convince themselves that their individual programs are a success, while at the same time there's been little or no change in the bigger picture. That's why you need to think through your key drivers, three-to-six-year outcomes, and six-to-ten-year outcomes. You have to think beyond the programmatic level of data and get at that bigger-picture data. So if your shared result is reducing carbon emissions by 25 percent, don't just track overall carbon emissions and the number of trees planted. What's the data in between that will build out your data-driven feedback loop?

 *Tools*

My colleague at Living Cities, JaNay Queen Nazaire, developed a useful tool to help you figure out what data you need to collect and how to get it.

The Data Inventory[21] has seven components:

1. Outcome Data: What data do you want? This component is a simple description of the data you need, like "employment rate" or "graduation rate."

2. Outcome Type: What kind of data is this? Is it an actual outcome that links to the overall impact of your work? Or is it more of a key driver that shows how your programs are doing?

3. Data Accessibility: How accessible are your data? Are they "accessible" (you have immediate access to the data), "available" (the data are available for access, but you have to do a little work or call on someone else to get them), or "aspirational" (you need/want the data but must create a way to get them)?

4. Data Source: Who collects the data? Which partners need to be engaged to access the data?

5. Timing of Data Collection: Quarterly? Yearly? Something else?

6. Challenges with Data: What stands in the way of or will hinder your data collection?

7.   Data Importance: How critical are these data to your work? Which should you prioritize?

By filling out the spreadsheet on page 67, you'll get a sense of what data exists already and what does not. You can then determine the next steps to get the data you need for your work, whether that's engaging with partners differently or finding new partners to work with.

Download this tool at http://tools.changeforimpact.org

OVERCOME YOUR DATA CHALLENGES

Data collection and data analysis within cross-sector partnerships is challenging to the private, public, and nonprofit sectors because of challenges unique to each of their working environments. Depending on which sector you are in, understanding these challenges—and overcoming them—will help equip you to change your organization to create lasting impact faster and more efficiently.

Nonprofit Sector's Challenge: Collecting Data

Most nonprofits have a basic problem with data infrastructure: collecting the data in the first place. They often do not have robust enough infrastructure to actually track data in a way that can be helpful to a collaborative.

This lack of capacity exists in the nonprofit sector for many reasons. Many funders do not fund what they see as "overhead" expenses, which is often what nonprofits actually need to fund data infrastructure. Funders also require nonprofits to collect certain types of data, which can take away from staff's time for collecting data that might be more relevant to their work. It is not just about the funders, though. Many nonprofit staff members feel that collecting and analyzing data is a detriment to their ability to serve clients, which is the true purpose of their work.

DATA INVENTORY

	OUTCOME DATA	OUTCOME TYPE	DATA AVAILABILITY	DATA SOURCE	TIMING OF DATA COLLECTION	CHALLENGES WITH DATA	DATA IMPORTANCE
EXPLANATION	This is a label for the data that will provide evidence on the outcome.	Key driver; 1-3 year outcome; 3-6 year outcome; 6-10 year population outcome.	Accessible data: have access now; Available data: can get access with easy steps; Aspirational data: need to figure out way to get.	Description of who collects the data or which partners need to be engaged to access the data; include url if available.	Description of how often the data are collected and made available.	This could be a description of challenges in accessing the data and/or challenges with the data themselves.	The prioritization level of the data.
DIRECTIONS	Write in.	Select from dropdown.	Select from dropdown.	Write in.	Select from dropdown.	Write in.	Select from dropdown.
EXAMPLE	Employment rate	3-6 year outcome	Accessible	http://www.labormar-ketinfo.edd.ca.gov/LMID/Quarterly_Workforce_Indicators.html	Quarterly	Only provides raw numbers of employed, not percent	Moderately Important

Private Sector's Challenge: Valuing Social Change beyond Dollars

The private sector's major challenge is tracking value beyond that of dollars earned or created. That isn't to say businesses only care about profit; most, if not all, businesses understand there is more to creating value than just profit. But typically, businesses are more comfortable measuring things such as revenue created from minority-owned small businesses or increased earnings from low-income people in a particular underresourced neighborhood.

Businesses can learn from nonprofits and government, both of which understand that change happens outside of traditional economic forces. Nonprofits and government tend to be more comfortable in agreeing to track more intangible factors, such as increased confidence in ability to secure a job or if a person feels safe in his or her community.

Private-sector engagement has been a challenge for many cross-sector partnerships, but creating a more inclusive data infrastructure system can help businesses become more involved in collective impact initiatives. For example, the Network for Economic Opportunity, discussed earlier, has created an outcomes framework that includes employment rates, with a clear link to economic activity. But the Network also wants to change enforcement policies, which may require businesses to get outside their comfort zone to understand how they can contribute.

Public Sector's Challenge: Measuring Impact, Not Outputs

The public sector's big challenge is to move beyond collecting data on outputs to managing data-tracking systems that they can show have impact on people's lives. Governments tend to be more comfortable working with data that show how well a program is doing what it is supposed to be doing, such as providing job referrals to unemployed residents. Many agencies already collect data on types of services provided and clients served, which are important data to have in collaborative work. But to know whether or not your cross-sector partnership is making broad, systems-level changes, it must build data infrastructure that can track impact, such as whether or not a high school graduate can actually earn a living.

Agreeing to track data on impact requires agencies to think on a bigger scale and potentially partner with other agencies or organizations. The bureaucracies within government agencies can make these larger-scale partnerships difficult and therefore create resistance from internal staff. There is also more external scrutiny of the public sector, which makes it culturally difficult to announce goals that may not be achieved in the short term.

If government can learn to think in terms of the scale of impact, this could open up a lot of opportunities. Recent work on Pay for Success (discussed later in chapter 6) has shown what happens when government begins focusing on impact rather than outcomes, creating a chain of continuous improvements.

WHAT'S NEXT: COLLABORATION

Now that you've learned how to change your organization, you're ready to move on to changing how you collaborate with others. You may have noticed throughout this chapter that a lot of the advice for your organization is also applicable to a cross-sector partnership. That's because every organization involved in a cross-sector partnership needs to shift how they do their work, not just yours.

The next two chapters focus on how to best structure a cross-sector partnership and how partners can best collaborate together. The final chapter discusses how you can better support collaboration to instill the lessons from this book to other organizations with which you work.

Looking Forward:
Change How Your Organization Works

Questions to consider:

- How are you harnessing the intrinsic motivation of your team?

- How can you model behavior, align resources, and catalyze change?

- How can you strengthen the feedback culture in your organization?

- Do you have a data-driven feedback loop? If not, how can you create one with your partners?

- Are you collecting the right data you need for your data-driven feedback loop?

CHAPTER 4

CHANGE HOW YOU COLLABORATE

When Living Cities created the Integration Initiative (TII) in 2010 to speed up the pace of social change, while widening its scale, we helped each member of the initiative incorporate four high-impact strategies into their work:

- Move beyond delivering programs and instead focus on transforming systems.

- Build a resilient civic infrastructure, with one "table" where decision-makers from across sectors and jurisdictions can formally convene and work together to define and address complex social problems (the framework we now call collective impact).

- Bring disruptive innovations into the mainstream and redirect funds away from obsolete approaches toward what works.

- Supplement traditional government and philanthropic funding streams by driving the private market to work on behalf of low-income people.

Four years later, Living Cities decided to shift the program design and expand the TII network. Because we had shifted how we thought about change, how we created change, and how our organization worked, we were able to make this shift toward collaborating in new and different ways. The new design for TII placed more emphasis on defining and achieving outcomes for low-income people. The shift created some questions among the various cities' initiatives about how to best go forward achieving their outcomes. It challenged them to take a closer look at the ways in which they were collaborating—and base their partnerships on shared interests that were sharpened into focused, well-defined shared results.

As discussed in chapter 3, having clearly defined, measureable goals acts like a powerful glue, holding cross-sector partnerships together. However, these partnerships have many other moving parts that can either enhance or minimize the impact they will have on communities and individual lives. Each cross-sector partnership needs to be intentionally structured to be able to achieve lasting impact. At Living Cities, one way we like to make sense of this structure is to compare building a cross-sector partnership to planning a wedding.

THE WEDDING PLANNING MODEL FOR SUCCESSFUL CROSS-SECTOR PARTNERSHIPS

If you've ever been involved in planning a wedding—whether your own, a friend's, or your child's—you're well aware that many factors combine to make a successful wedding. In a similar way, most cross-sector partnerships have greater potential for success when they are well organized. Using wedding planning as our model, Living Cities came up with some ideas for how to change the way you collaborate with your partners so that together you can create a lasting impact. (Much of this chapter draws on the work of former Living Cities employee Alison Gold, who has since moved on to the Presidio Institute. I encourage you to check out her work as well.)

What's the Shared Result?

A wedding has a goal: usually to celebrate the love of two people for one another and for guests to have a great time—but how everyone involved defines that is not always the same. Imagine that the groom's goal is a simple, intimate wedding to celebrate what he believes is a private moment between his partner and him, while his partner's mother wants to have a huge guest list in order to impress as many of her business colleagues as possible. These two contributors to the wedding plan will be working at cross purposes—and sometimes the same sort of thing can happen with cross-sector partnerships.

In the same way that the people planning a wedding need to come together to agree on a goal for a wedding, so do cross-sector partners need to agree on their purpose. The end result that everyone is working toward is far bigger than any single person's interests. When you have several organizations that are all sharing the same result, their common result is also bigger than any smaller goals the separate groups might have. All their resources can work together toward the common objective. It's that larger, shared result that truly matters. The shared result of a data-driven feedback loop can be thought of as an organization or a cross-sector partnership's "North Star" for everything they do.

So let's say an organization has a goal of reducing unemployment in its community by 10 percent by 2020. Right now that 10 percent equals thirty thousand people who are out of work. The organization has an amazing program that has found jobs for a hundred people, and that's great—but they need to ask themselves, "How do those one hundred jobs contribute to the larger shared result of thirty thousand?"

Obviously, that one organization will never be able to get there by itself. They need to ask, "What other resources do we need to reach our shared result? What information, political capital, and financial capital do we need to bring to the table to achieve the result we want?" When human lives are involved, it's difficult to be logical about picking one step to tackle first and then moving on to the next one. The components of the data-driven feedback loop help organizations and cross-sector partnerships prioritize and sequence their work to create the highest level of impact.

This is true in both the private sector and the social sector. I learned this firsthand when my company acquired a mortgage bank in Mexico City. Not only did we have to contend with the cultural differences between our company and the mortgage bank, but we also had to navigate the differences between business approaches in the United States and Mexico. And even though aligning very different cultures has no playbook that works the same in every acquisition, I had a clear goal, guidelines, and a deadline. That clarity helped my team sequence our efforts over time.

Our partners in HOPE SF, an initiative in the city of San Francisco focused on transforming distressed public housing, understand the importance of relying on a shared result to prioritize what comes first in large-scale change efforts. In the early stages of the effort, the foundation community and private sector led most of the project management and investment. But over time, public sector leadership wanted to do more. How could they change the way they worked to ensure that what they were learning from HOPE SF could benefit low-income people of color across the city? Around this time, HOPE SF became a member of the Integration Initiative. With support from Living Cities, the HOPE SF cross-sector leaders set a new shared result and deadline—quadrupling the number of (formerly) public housing households of color that are thriving within the city by 2020. Like most communities across the country, there are many different disparities that the city's people of color are contending with, including housing, health, and education.

The following chart gives a graphical representation of HOPE SF's work and how they have sequenced out the steps they need to achieve. This graphic shows both the strategies they will deliver, as well as the data they are going to track to make sure they are achieving what they set out to achieve (these are the key drivers, three-to-six-year outcomes, and six-to-ten-year outcomes described in chapter 3).

Tools

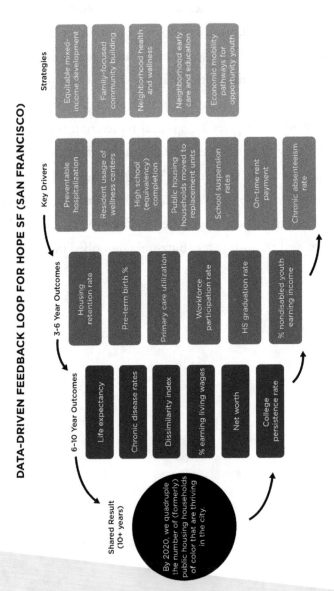

DATA-DRIVEN FEEDBACK LOOP FOR HOPE SF (SAN FRANCISCO)

Strategies
- Equitable mixed-income development
- Family-focused community building
- Neighborhood health and wellness
- Neighborhood early care and education
- Economic mobility pathways for opportunity youth

Key Drivers
- Preventable hospitalization
- Resident usage of wellness centers
- High school (equivalency) completion
- Public housing households moved to replacement units
- School suspension rates
- On-time rent payment
- Chronic absenteeism rate

3-6 Year Outcomes
- Housing retention rate
- Pre-term birth %
- Primary care utilization
- Workforce participation rate
- HS graduation rate
- % nondisabled youth earning income

6-10 Year Outcomes
- Life expectancy
- Chronic disease rates
- Dissimilarity index
- % earning living wages
- Net worth
- College persistence rate

Shared Result (10+ years)
- By 2020, we quadruple the number of (formerly) public housing households of color that are thriving in the city.

The diagram illustrates well-defined shared goals for an initiative in San Francisco that is working to eliminate disparities for families that use public housing services.

Download this tool at http://tools.changeforimpact.org

DEFINING A SHARED RESULT

The most important part of the data-driven feedback loop, and where we spent a lot of time working with the HOPE SF leadership and other partners, is the shared result. Establishing a clear, well-defined shared result makes the rest of the data-driven feedback loop possible.

The shared result helps equip the individual with what she needs to change her organization. If you have placed a hundred people into jobs, and your organization's goal was ninety-nine, then your team would rightfully celebrate. But if your organization is part of a cross-sector partnership and your shared result is thirty thousand, then you would celebrate your progress while recognizing that collectively there was much more work to do. Relying on the lessons to change how you create change in chapter 2, you can use a shared result to define how leaders must change themselves and their organizations to achieve the shared result of the cross-sector partnership.

Living Cities has identified four components of effective shared results that will unify a cross-sector partnership and drive it toward success.

1. ***Have a population-level focus.*** The shared result of any cross-sector partnership should be tied to achieving a "population-level" result. A "population-level" focus means the result isn't specifically tied to one program. For example, "increase job referrals through our program" wouldn't be considered a population-level shared result, because success only depends on the efforts of one organization leading one program (even if that program involves multiple stakeholders). In contrast, "reduce unemployment in our city" is a population-level shared result because it depends on the efforts of many actors, and achieving it will have an impact on an entire population of people. (It's okay to

have a geographic scope to your shared result, such as a city or region, as long as it's not too narrowly defined to constrain the impact of your initiative.)

One thing to consider for your cross-sector partnership is whether you need a single shared result—or multiple shared results that tie in to a broader mission or vision. We've seen initiatives approach this question in both ways. The right answer for you will depend on the local context of your work. For example, the Communities of Opportunity initiative in King County, WA, is working to close the gaps in health disparities. They've come up with three different shared results that focus on economics, connection to a community, and housing.

2. ***Make it SMART: Specific, Measurable, Attainable, Relevant, and Time-Bound***. This means your cross-sector partnership's shared result must have some sort of metric attached to it and an element of time. Your shared result can't be merely a motivational statement, such as, "We want everybody to be healthy." That's good for a vision and a rallying cry, but you must be able to determine if you're actually achieving your goal.

    So, for example, don't say, "Our goal is to reduce unemployment." Instead, say, "Our goal is to reduce unemployment in Anyville, USA, by 50 percent over ten years." This has a specific focus (unemployment in a specific city); it is measurable (50 percent decrease) and attainable (it may seem like a big undertaking, but is possible); it is relevant to the work of creating lasting impact; and it's time-bound (ten years). Making a shared result SMART helps cross-sector partnership narrow in on exactly what they want to achieve with their work. Once this specificity is set, it becomes easier to figure out how to get the work done and who needs to be involved.

We've found that cross-sector partnerships often confuse "specific" with "program-focused." Making a shared result specific does not require focusing on a specific program or service. Instead, cross-sector partnerships should be focused on population-level results. A shared result of "increasing job referrals by 15 percent in five years through our program" fails the test of "relevant" in SMART because it doesn't have a population-level result.

Making a shared result "attainable" is also more of an art than a science. Cross-sector partnerships often confuse attainable with "helping us all continue business as usual." So if five programs each place one hundred people in jobs annually, then it is easy to set the shared result at five hundred. But if the number of unemployed in your city is ten thousand, then five hundred employed is not nearly enough to achieve the change you seek. This is where bright spots come in, as discussed in chapter 2. Look within your city, your region, your country, even the world and search for where employment is working really well. Because wherever and whenever your goal is working somewhere else, it shows you what is truly attainable even if from where you sit it feels impossible. Your SMART goal should have a "gulp" factor that will push you to solutions that will make your partnership greater than the sum of its parts.

3. ***Ensure all partners agree and share accountability.*** Making a shared result SMART may seem straightforward,

but the challenge comes when partners must commit to holding themselves accountable to achieving that result. For example, one cross-sector partnership we support undertook an intensive planning process with the members of their cross-sector partnership. They thought they had come to an agreement on a shared result, but when they moved into implementing their strategies, they realized that their partners were not fully committed. They had to go back and revise their shared result to ensure their partners had fully committed themselves to the initiative.

4. *Ground the shared result in local context.* You must engage organizational partners in defining the shared result, and you also need to think about the needs of your community when creating the shared result. Cross-sector partnerships can sometimes agree to shared results that are not in sync with community needs. For example, you may think unemployment is the major issue in your community, but it could actually be a lack of public transportation connecting people to places of work. Or cross-sector partnerships may be required to design a shared result in a specific way because of outside funders or other requirements. A great example of aligning a shared result to community needs is our Integration Initiative partners in New Orleans, LA, the Network for Economic Opportunity. City leaders were motivated to support their residents who were still reeling from the aftermath of Hurricane Katrina. They developed a comprehensive plan including housing, criminal justice reform, and health care. But when they checked in with their residents they were advised again and again that

the number-one issue was unemployment. And based on this feedback, they changed their approach to focus predominantly on increasing employment, particularly for African American men, who had the highest rates of unemployment in the city.

New Orleans provides a great example of why it is important to ensure your shared result responds to community needs, actively engages community members in the planning process (as discussed in chapter 2), or includes community groups as full partners of the initiative.

Once you set your shared result with your partners, the next step is to set up a series of metrics over time (make sure they're all SMART!) to give you the feedback you need to track your progress. These different metrics will help you build out the rest of your data-driven feedback loop by establishing those key drivers, three-to-six-year outcomes, and six-to-ten-year outcomes. The next challenge will be making sure you've got the right data to track toward your shared result.

Who Do You Invite?

Now that you've got the shared result for your wedding, it's time to move on to the guest list. If you're drawing up the guest list for a wedding, you'll probably think carefully about who you want to be there. Which people will contribute most to your overall goals for this special day? Do you want to include business associates—or only your closest friends? Do you want to invite your great-aunts and great-uncles, along with your second-cousins-once-removed—or do you want to stick to family members with whom you have genuine close relationships? There's no single correct answer to these questions.

Since each couple's wedding is different from any other, whom they'll decide to invite will be a decision that's uniquely theirs, as well. The one thing that's certain: your wedding guests won't be just a random group of people you picked by saying eeny-meeny-miny-mo with all the various friends, family members, and colleagues you know.

BE INTENTIONAL ABOUT YOUR PARTNERS

The same thing is true when choosing whom to involve in a cross-sector partnership. Sometimes, people think, *Oh, okay, we want a cross-sector group of leaders*—and then they use a "Noah's Ark" approach, randomly picking people to represent the public sector, the private sector, and the social sector.

Another mistake folks sometimes make is thinking of people they already know from each of the sectors. "Joe's a nice guy, he's a CEO, and I know he thinks like we do, so he'd be great to have at the table." Or, "Let's ask Mary from local government because she's my next-door-neighbor, and she and I have so much in common." Well, that's great, as long as Joe and Mary are in positions where they have capital and influence to help you reach your goals. But if your goal is to decrease childhood obesity in local schools by 50 percent by 2020, and Joe is the CEO of an engineering company and Mary is the railroad commissioner, it's possible they might not be the people you need at your table. You might all have a nice time sitting around the table talking—but how much will you be able to accomplish? Achieving a shared result needs to be what drives your choices, more than any already-established relationships.

Other times, there's a common "enemy" that pulls everyone together. Say the city government plans to pull down some historical buildings in order to construct a mall. Community residents, local business owners, property owners, school officials, and the faith community may all have their reasons for not wanting a mall plopped down in their neighborhood. When they come together to fight the city, their passion may be a great uniting factor—but they may not have anyone involved who will actually be able to drive a policy change. When it comes to cross-sector partnerships, you can sit around a table, all singing the same song from the same hymnbook, for a long, long time without ever accomplishing anything.

PUT THE RESULTS AT THE CENTER

So when it is time to pick the people at your table, put the results you hope to achieve at the center, the same way you would if you were planning a wedding. We use a diagram as a tool for achieving the best combination of people in a cross-sector partnership. This is called a "results at the center diagram" and draws from the Anne E. Casey Foundation (among others) work on results-based leadership.

Let's say your central goal is to reduce obesity rates in your city by 10 percent by 2025. That's the goal that will be at the center of your cross-sector partnership. It's the shared result you will all be working toward. Now you need to ask, "Who is in a position of authority and control to help make this happen? Who has the skill sets we'll need to better understand this problem? Who has capital to spend to help us reach our goal?"

Make sure you don't focus only on one of those questions. Don't make the mistake of bringing together a bunch of community health workers and no one else. They may have the skills you need—but they're not in positions of power where they'll be able to help you change the policies that cause economic health disparities. You're going to need someone from the public sector at your table who has the power to actually shape and change government policy.

Tools

RESULTS AT THE CENTER

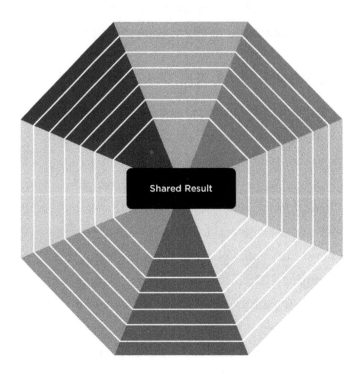

Here's how you can use the "results at the center" tool:

- First, write down your stated result in the center section. (Make sure it's focused on people! For more on why, check out chapter 2.)

- Next, label each colored section based on the different groups of people who will be able to help your partnership reach its goals, such as community leaders, business CEOs, government officials, nonprofit directors, or people from the faith community.

- Then, write on the lines within each colored section names of specific organizations that fit into those categories. Those organizations with more influence on the result should be placed closer to the center of the diagram.

Download this tool at http://tools.changeforimpact.org

By the same token, however, don't gather a group only from your municipal government; they may have the power to change policy, but they won't always understand the nuances of the problem. Any policy changes they make won't be shaped by people who are on the ground, dealing with the problem day to day. Just as big a mistake would be to gather a group of business leaders who have the funds you need but who don't really care about the shared result at the center of your partnership. They may even be thinking to themselves, *If this policy around school lunches is changed, it will negatively affect my bottom line, so I'm going to drag my feet as much as I can.* You need to bring together the skills, the will, and the power, all brought together to drive the long-term impact you want to see.

DON'T INVITE JUST THE USUAL SUSPECTS

When you're deciding whom to include in a cross-sector partnership, try thinking outside of the box you're accustomed to using. For example, every initiative needs funding, but you may be able to get it from unexpected sources. Don't assume that grants are the only option. For example, Kresge Foundation wanted to increase access to health services for one hundred thousand patients. Instead of relying only on funding nonprofits through grants, which is the usual way foundations try to solve problems, they decided to invest in health service companies. Kresge will invest up to $5 million in companies to support them in serving more customers.[22] Because these funds are not grants, the investment will be recovered and can be dedicated to other opportunities in the future. You can learn more about different ways to resource your collaboration in chapter 6.

Living Cities found an unexpected partner in LinkedIn. The social media site was able to provide another necessary resource—information—through their sharing of employment data to the public sector for free. This data is far richer and more meaningful than what we can get from the US Bureau of Labor Statistics, because as a social media site, LinkedIn can spot trends really quickly. At the touch of a button, they can tell us, "These are the jobs that people are getting, these are the jobs people are applying for, and these are the types of people who are moving into your area or not moving into your area." Their numbers may only apply to about 60 percent of the total population, but they still are a valuable addition to our data-driven employment initiatives.[23]

If you were working to decrease unemployment, though, LinkedIn probably wouldn't be the first place you'd think of to go for help. It certainly wasn't for us. Instead, odds are good you'd say, "All right, let me go to our workforce investment board," "Let me go to the Department of Labor," or, "Let me go to our office of economic development." Those are all good sources of information, and you'll need their data for long-term credibility. But always keep your mind open to new possibilities. Take advantage of every possible source of will, information, and capital that might be out there.

Another possibility might be that you enlist the partners you already have to work together in a different way from what they've always done previously. For example, instead of having a social-sector agency drive a collaborative initiative, someone from the private sector might be able to act as the convening organization.

Case Study

CAMPBELL SOUP

Campbell Soup Company is a great example of looking beyond usual suspects to create a cross-sector partnership. This private-sector company has implemented a ten-year, $10 million initiative to reduce childhood obesity and hunger in the city of Camden, NJ, through its Healthy Communities program. Building on its work in Camden, the company plans to expand into other cities around the country where it has a business presence.

Kim Fortunato, now the President of the Campbell Soup Foundation, told the Collective Impact Forum that the company has a "long-standing commitment to social responsibility, to help deliver both sustainability and business results. We believe that giving back to the communities where we live and work is part of our DNA."[24]

Campbell Soup has done a good job defining its shared result—reducing childhood obesity and hunger in the city of Camden by 50 percent in ten years—and the company under-stands that it needs to enlist many players in order to take on such a complex issue. The company has also embedded the goal in their business strategy, which focuses on aligning Campbell Soup with health and well-being, so that the initiative will have long-term sustainability.

Food access was another priority in Campbell Soup's strategy for reaching the collaborative's central goal. As the ini-tiative got started, the leaders brought together funders who were already putting money into food-access issues in Camden. Sitting around the table together, it became clear that funders were investing money where they thought there was a need but without much evidence to indicate the most effective use of capital. This lead to the initiative's next step: they called in a food-access expert to help them invest purposefully in a way that would align with their goal.

As they went to work, Campbell Soup was careful not to brand the initiative with their name. Instead, they wanted to offer the entire food industry a model that could inspire others to get involved. The company was focused on doing something bigger than themselves.

Businesses don't usually think of getting involved all by themselves, however, in the way that Campbell Soup did. Since they're usually not used to thinking in terms of a larger, intrinsically motivated agenda, nonprofits will probably need to make the case to companies if they want them involved in a cross-sector partnership. If you represent a nonprofit or government agency and want to engage with a business, you may get farther in a conversation with business leaders if you can change the narrative from, "I want you to write a big check to help our cause," to, "Will you look at complex issues with a diverse group of leaders and figure out how to make meaningful change?"

I've adapted Miller Heiman's "strategic selling" guide[25] to develop a framework to help nonprofits and government understand the private-sector stakeholders who secure partnerships for their organization. Each has access to different resources, and therefore a different role to play in managing and deepening partnerships with the private sector:[26]

The economic buyer. This is the ultimate decision-maker, who has the power to release funds or kill the partnership; it's usually one person but can also be a board. Economic buyers ask questions about overall strategy. To ensure that your partnership remains an organizational priority, use quarterly check-ins that focus on both the business and mission outcomes that result from the partnership.

The user buyer. This person actually uses or supervises your talent or service, or otherwise stands to directly benefit from your partnership with the business. They are important to the lasting success of a partnership and judge the service based on the impact it will have on their specific duties. Because they're the ones you will interact with most, effective engagement should include weekly to biweekly check-ins to gather ongoing feedback and proactively address concerns.

The technical buyer. This is the gatekeeper, who often has the ability to say no to the partnership (often human resource, legal, or finance staff). They embed the partnership in the actual operations of any business partner and ensure that the partnership meets organizational criteria and requirements.

The coach—your champion within the business, who helps navigate the partnership. The coach is the ally and advocate of your program or services. They should be at a peer level or above with the economic buyer and should provide the guidance they need to navigate the business's cultural and political dynamics.

 *Tools*

ENGAGE THESE FOUR STAKEHOLDERS TO CREATE PRIVATE-SECTOR PARTNERSHIPS

Buyer	Example Title/Dept.	Key Role	Messaging
Economic	Leadership–C-suite for smaller/local organizations, regional/business unit executive for larger organizations	Key to resources for the partnership	Aligns with budget Return on investment Productivity Profitability
User	Manager of related service or product	Key to the lasting success of the partnership	Reliability Increased efficiency Better performance Easier alternative
Technical	Human resources, legal, finance	Key to embedding the partnerships	Meets requirements Reliability Discounts/price
Coach	Company board member, CSR, nonprofit board member (at peer level with economic buyer)	Key to navigating the partnership	Recognition Visibility Seen as problem solver

Adopted from Miller Heiman's "strategic selling" guide.

Download this tool at http://tools.changeforimpact.org

When nonprofits and businesses work together, they'll probably discover that part of their cultural differences have to do with vocabulary. They'll each be unfamiliar with the terminology the other uses. What's to be done about this?

SPEAK A COMMON LANGUAGE
AROUND THE TABLE

Imagine you're planning a wedding where the family of one of the marriage partners speaks only Mandarin Chinese, while some members of the other's family speak English and some are most comfortable speaking Spanish. If you want to make sure that everyone has a good time, then you'll need to take into account the language differences. You may need to send out invitations in more than one language. You might have translators at the actual wedding to interpret the toasts. When it comes to cross-sector partnerships, you can run into similar problems. You may all be speaking English— but that doesn't mean that you're using the same terms for the same concepts.

Campbell Soup's experience with the Healthy Communities program is a good illustration of the way in which the people around a table may all speak slightly different languages. The Healthy Communities program was using the collective impact model described in chapter 2, and its leadership found that when they talked about collective impact to the people within Campbell Soup, they communicated more effectively if they used the term "change management" instead. The marketing department, for example, was totally familiar with the concept—but they were accustomed to using different terminology for it.

You'll see the same sort of thing if you look at the language describing collective impact used by FSG, the consulting firm that originally came up with the terminology—and then compare it to the terminology we use at Living Cities, or what's on StriveTogether's website, another pioneer of the collective impact model. While we use different language, we've put in the time with each other to understand each of our different approaches. FSG's initial language was generic and theoretical. StriveTogether's language is practitioner focused and specifically for education. Living Cities' language is generic and practitioner focused. The time we've invested with each other allows us to have shared *understanding* that supports shared *action*. Think about it this way: My best friend is from Ohio, and I think it's weird that she calls soda "pop." My husband is from Atlanta, and I think it's weird that he calls soda "coke." But when either of them is thirsty, I understand what they need to get the right drink.

If you are embarking on a collaborative change process, you need to do five important things.

First, you need to **form strong relationships** at the beginning of the process to understand the language others use; we can't just work together in name only. Communication becomes a whole lot easier when it's between people who genuinely like or at least respect each other.

Second, you need to **be willing to be flexible** in the way that you communicate. It's easy to fall into the trap of being patronizing when you're trying to support changing behavior; you may say to yourself, *I just don't know how many times I can explain the same concepts to people to get them to understand me.* Before you gallop off on that high horse, remember that changing behavior is more about changing hearts and minds than about drilling definitions into people's brains. If people can grasp the concepts, then the words they use to describe them really don't matter.

Third, **recognize the culture of the people with whom you're working**. They're not lab rats, passively sitting there while you do something to them; instead, they are active participants in the problem-solving process. That means you need to use language that resonates with them. Simpler words may be more effective than jargon. Remember, the tool you're using—whether we call it systems change, collective impact, or something else—really doesn't matter. What matters is that you truly achieve a lasting impact.

Fourth, as Stephen M. R. Covey so articulately said, **change moves at the speed of trust**. At Living Cities, we've learned that we can more effectively catalyze change when we have trusted people on our side who can serve in the role of translator. These are people who give us credibility because they have the respect or trust of other leaders. When they communicate alongside us, they make it clear that they're not talking about something that's theoretical and abstract; their language is grounded in practical experience.

Last, **we need to be willing to communicate in a different way as many times as we need to**. At Living Cities, our language started out inside a small team. It evolved over lunches and around staff-meeting tables, and then we tested it at external conferences and on webinars. Each iteration helps us make sure that our discussions are focused more on the changes we're seeking and less on the tool we're using.

Ultimately, it doesn't matter what we call whatever approach we're using—collective impact, collaborative change, community change, cross-sector collaboration, who cares? What matters is this: Does it work? Does it help us see what we need to do to reach our shared goal?

WHAT'S ON YOUR TO-DO LIST?

To go back to our wedding analogy, once you have your guest list drawn up, there are still plenty more tasks to do before the big day arrives. You'll need to locate a venue, meet with an officiant, find a florist, buy the right clothes . . . and the list goes on and on. If you try to do everything all at once, you'll get frustrated and overwhelmed. You also probably don't have an unlimited budget, so you may need to carefully plan what you're going to pay for when. Your ultimate goal is still the same—you want to create a special day to celebrate the love between two people—but you'll need to prioritize the necessary steps you need to take to reach your goal. The same is true when it comes to working with a cross-sector partnership to bring about a lasting impact on your community.

The Communities of Opportunity, the health-focused cross-sector partnership from King County, WA, brought a broad group of stakeholders connected to the work at a lot of different levels in the community, including the Seattle Foundation, county officials, and the Public Health Department. Because they brought everybody they needed at their table for the skills, the influence, and the will, they were able to get off to a great start as a strong coalition of willing people working hard for a common goal.

Sometimes, however, your greatest strength can also be a potential weakness. When you have a cross-sector group of people who all care passionately about their goal, there's a tendency to want to tackle everything at once. Each person has a unique perspective that makes him or her feel that a specific sub-goal should be targeted first. If the group is working to fight obesity, for example, one member may say, "But what about tobacco use? You can't say that obesity is more important than tobacco as a threat to health!"

You don't want your group to break down over prioritizing your objectives, so you need to keep your attention firmly fixed on the central goal that unites you. What can you do first that will move you closer to that goal? What will give you the most momentum? Don't start out with something that has the highest barriers to success; wait to tackle that until you have more power behind you. Instead, maybe there's work already in motion that you can piggyback on to help get you moving more quickly. Are there three focal areas you can prioritize that everyone will agree on? Getting quick wins at the start of your partnership can help build momentum and get people more engaged.

In King County, the cross-sector group has created an initiative called Best Starts for Kids, which is working to improve the county's health and well-being by investing in prevention and early intervention for children, youth, families, and communities. It's funded by a tax that will generate about $65 million per year, while costing the average King County property owner just a little more than a dollar per week. It's a comprehensive approach to early childhood development, starting with prenatal support, then working to sustain that gain through the teenage years, and also investing in healthy, safe communities that reinforce progress. It's a great way for them to gain momentum toward their central goal. Each cross-sector group will need to handle prioritization differently, depending in part on who is on the "guest list."

Sometimes, you may not be able to immediately achieve the ideal balance of players around your table. Our partners in Baltimore, called the Baltimore Integration Partnership, have at different times focused on policy, workforce development, local hiring, and housing in service of supporting low-income people in their city. For each focus, they've shifted around the players at their table. Successes in each area have allowed them to tackle new and different challenges.

QUESTIONS TO HELP DETERMINE STRUCTURE

Many cross-sector partnerships struggle to achieve the shared result they've identified as their goal. These partnerships face many challenges, but one of the most difficult struggles relates to building the right structure and bringing in the right partners to the partnership. So what questions should you and your partners be asking and answering to set your cross-sector partnership on a path to success?

Based on the wedding-planning analogy, Living Cities has identified four questions.

Question 1: What is the shared result that your cross-sector partnership is trying to achieve?

Creating a shared result—described earlier in this chapter—is the critical first step in forming any cross-sector partnership. Get clear on that shared result first, and *then* build the partnership from there. Don't try to do it the other way around. This can mean the difference between a vague goal like, "We want to decrease unemployment," and a much more specific goal such as, "Ninety percent of the labor force will be employed by the year 2020."

Question 2: What would a map or chart of your cross-sector partnership's structure need to look like to achieve its shared result?

At a wedding, the seating chart creates a structure for the whole event and helps guests understand where they belong. In building the seating chart, the hosts aim to design a structure that will support the overall goal (that is, celebrating love and partying). They seat guests with other people they'll enjoy, since fun at a table contributes to the fun of the whole group. At the same time, however, the guests aren't stuck at their table all night; they're circulating and connecting with other guests on the dance floor, talking to one another, visiting the restroom, or hitting the dessert buffet.

When it comes to a cross-sector partnership, creating a "seating chart" can manifest in many ways, so long as it helps to document and solidify the relationships between the partners, similar to the way in which a wedding planner creates place settings for the guests. Cross-sector partnerships might establish procedures and processes;

articulate differentiated roles and commitments; and create operating documents, memorandum of understanding, contracts, or other documentation. All these are in effect their "seating chart," providing a structure that supports the partnership's overall goals.[27]

 *Tools*

WEDDING SEATING CHART FOR CROSS-SECTOR PARTNERSHIPS

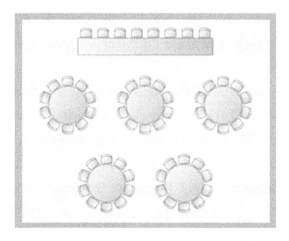

Filling out this mock wedding seating chart can help you structure your cross-sector partnership.

Download this tool at http://tools.changeforimpact.org

Question 3: How do partners plug into the different components of your cross-sector partnership?

At a wedding, the vision and execution of the event is steered by the individuals with authority—usually those getting married (or maybe those paying the bill). However, everyone involved with the wedding party, from the guests to the officiant to the caterers to the band, has distinct roles and responsibilities for making the event successful. At the same time, not every person is well suited for every role or every position on the dance floor. Would you have a distant cousin that you haven't seen in a decade choose the wedding rings? Would you want your obnoxious Uncle Fred to be the best man? Would you seat the newlyweds at different tables in the back corners of the room? Of course not! None of those would go over well. They're such bad ideas that they're ludicrous.

In cross-sector partnership, however, members can sometimes end up in roles for which they are not at all suited. As with a wedding, achieving success is dependent on the appropriate individuals contributing in the appropriate ways. Different individuals fill different roles in an organization and therefore contribute differently to your partnership. A CEO of a major employer can achieve one set of objectives, while an HR manager from that same company will be able to accomplish quite different things—so they need to be plugged into the partnership accordingly. By the same token, various organizations can be best utilized in specific ways. A large law firm will be able to contribute to your shared results in quite different ways from a faith community that is also part of your partnership. Each has something unique and valuable to offer—but if you put them in the wrong roles, what would have otherwise been a valuable contribution to the partnership's overall success can turn into a hindrance or even a cause for failure.

Question 4: How do you need to refine your cross-sector partnership to support success as your work evolves?

The best-planned weddings don't always work out quite as we intended. Your outdoor wedding by the ocean could become impossible if a thunderstorm rolls in. One of your groomspeople could suddenly become ill, the venue you'd planned on might have a fire that means you can't use it after all, or a bride may wake up with a bad case of poison ivy. These can all seem like disasters that will prevent the wedding's goals from being achieved—and yet with enough flexibility (and possibly antihistamine if the bride is covered with a rash), the wedding can still be a fun celebration of love.

I know this firsthand. In preparation for my wedding, I had PowerPoints, spreadsheets, clear roles, and commitment to our shared result (a great time celebrating our love) with my fiancé. And despite all that meticulous planning, Hurricane Charlie kept half of our guests from attending, and power outages killed my stored flowers and put our hairdressers out of commission. How did we respond? It was dicey for a few moments, but to this day our friends (and we) say it's the best wedding they ever attended!

When it comes to handling a cross-sector partnership, managing changing circumstances can be one of your greatest challenges. You've taken the time to map out the players and get them to work together, but as the work evolves, you may need to make some changes. As you refine your understanding of the problem you are trying to solve, some partners may not fit into the partnership in the same way, or you may learn you need others to join.

In the same way that you may need to find a last-minute venue for your all-outdoor wedding because of an impending thunderstorm, a cross-sector partnership may have to shift from its original plan. These shifts may be as hard as trying to fit two hundred wet people into the local church, but in the end, all that matters is that you achieve your goals. All that really must happen at a wedding is that two people celebrate their love with their friends and family; *how* that happens—outdoors or indoors, with one groomsperson or another—really doesn't matter, so long as the ultimate goal is accomplished. The same is true for your cross-sector partnership. If you successfully achieve your shared result, then it doesn't really matter if you got there using your original plan or an adapted version of it.

 **Share Your Story**

What have you learned in building your cross-sector partnership? Visit **www.changeforimpact.org** to tell us how you used this book to create lasting impact and Living Cities may highlight your work!

IMPLICATIONS OF CHANGING THE WAY YOU COLLABORATE

I came to Living Cities because I wanted to be part of an organization that was working to bridge the opportunity gaps faster than ever before. I've learned that no single individual, institution, or sector can alone achieve the pace and scale of impact that I want to see. As a result, we're not competing against other organizations. We're competing against far larger enemies—the factors that create the opportunity gaps in our society, things like poverty and hopelessness. In order to achieve our goals, we must not only form new partnerships—collaborating in ways we've never done before—but we must also begin to work together differently.

Looking Forward:
Change How You Collaborate

Questions to consider:

- Does your partnership have an established, SMART, people-focused shared result?

- Do you have a set of partners established that connect to your people-focused result?

- Do each of your partners understand the language and words that other partners regularly use?

- Do you have an established structure of roles and responsibilities for your cross-sector partnership?

- Does everyone know his or her role within that structure?

- Are people who have the power to make decisions represented in your cross-sector partnership?

- Do you know the next time the organizational make-up of your cross-sector partnership will be revisited?

CHAPTER 5

CHANGE HOW YOUR COLLABORATIVE DOES ITS WORK

As I have supported leaders in achieving lasting impact throughout my career, I've been struck sometimes by how bogged down people sometimes get during the process. People start arguing over who should be at the table, what is the right level of data, and even over what each step is called. In the course of sorting through this messiness, many get confused or, in the worst-case scenarios, discouraged.

In the face of all that confusion and discouragement, I want to say as clearly as I can that I have an unyielding belief that the problems our country faces are not only solvable, but the tools also exist to achieve them. What that tool is doesn't really matter to me. The tools aren't what drive me. What drives me are the reasons why we wield them— to close the opportunity gaps that too many people face.

One of the first things I did when I joined Living Cities was poke fun at how we often apply the wrong tools to the problems we face.

My colleague at Living Cities, Nadia Owusu, drew this comic to illustrate how we can sometimes apply a tool or an approach (in this case, collective impact) to the wrong kind of problem.

While this comic might make light of the challenges of social change, success is the right tool meeting the right solution. So with that goal in mind, I want to share with you several sets of tools that I have found useful to change how collaboratives work together to create lasting impact: collective problem solving, A3 problem solving, Results-Based Accountability (RBA), open-sourcing change, and the Bermuda Triangle of Cross-Sector Partnerships. Each of these tool sets have several components that will help collaboratives change the way they work.

USE COLLECTIVE PROBLEM SOLVING

During our first round of the Integration Initiative, our multicity cohort of cross-sector partnerships, we spent a lot of time telling people that we didn't want to invest in programs. People weren't too sure what we meant by that, and we soon found that it would probably have been easier to rip an infant from the arms of a mother than to stop a program once it has been funded. After all, a whole bunch of smart people worked hard to get a program funded by sharing their extensive research on why and how it would fix whatever wrong they were seeking to right. Unfortunately, when these programs begin showing themselves to be less effective, the work it took to get the resources to support the program in the first place can often create a backlash that hamstrings leadership in the future.

What we should have been saying was that we were looking for hypotheses to be tested rather than carved-in-stone solutions in the form of established programs. A solution that turns out to be wrong is considered a failure—but by their very definition, hypotheses are not solutions and must be constantly tested. This gives our cross-sector partnerships the freedom to fail in service of finding what works.

But to get people to a point of thinking about hypotheses to be tested rather than established programs as needed solutions, you must invest in collective problem solving. Collective problem solving is the process a collaborative, cross-sector partnership uses to address a complex problem and determine a potential solution. We think of it as a cycle with four stages: problem defining, interpreting and hypothesizing, solution finding, and analyzing and reflecting. This framework was developed through the work of former Living Cities employee Alison Gold but draws on the work of many different organizational development scholars across sectors.[28]

STAGE	DEFINITION	ACTIVITIES
Problem-Defining	*Observing events and patterns to gain greater insight into the source and nature of challenges.*	• Using diverse knowledge-including lived experience and local data, as well as national and international data—to understand and clearly define the problem. • Reconciling when data and lived experiences are in conflict • Naming the problem the partnership is trying to address.
Interpreting & Hypothesizing	*Interpreting what has been observed, and then developing hypotheses about what needs to change in order to yield different results.*	• Incorporating new ideas into thinking and letting go of out-of-date or discredited ideas. • Hypothesizing about how the world is working and what is causing the problem. • Developing a plausible understanding of the world in which to test solutions.
Solution-Finding	*Identifying and testing solutions to a recognized problem.*	• Recognizing the need to paint a vision for the future. • Identifying lots of potential solutions. • Developing projects, programs, and policies to test possible solutions in the realms of policy, practice, and funding streams.
Analyzing & Reflecting	*Determining if the solutions are effective and learning from them to gain a better understanding of the problem and the solutions that are needed to achieve the partnership's intended result.*	• Reflecting on the impact of tested solutions by comparing what was expected to what actually occurred. • Identifying what must be learned about the world to improve future solutions and outcomes. • Generating new hypotheses. • Restarting the cycle.

This chart comes from What Barriers? Insights from Solving Problems through Cross-Sector Partnerships, *by Alison Gold*

Although ideally, all collaboratives would fully engage in all four stages, the reality is that most partnerships tend to focus on some stages of the cycle more than others. For example, in the Minneapolis–St. Paul Itasca Project, currently involved with our Integration Initiative work in that region, a small set of leaders wanted business executives to get more involved in issues of regional importance. They conducted interviews with seventy to eighty CEOs to get a better sense of why business executives weren't engaged. These interviews helped with the first stage of the problem-solving cycle: defining the problem.

The next stage of the cycle focuses on interpreting what has been observed—and then developing hypotheses about what must change in order to yield different results. To do this, you need leaders who are willing to accept the data you have and then commit to changing behavior based on that data. Sometimes consultants are helpful as messengers to interpret data in ways that won't be as skewed by politics. Former Itasca Director Allison Barmann, who now is a vice president at the Bush Foundation, notes that the Itasca Project has been able to leverage consultants, such as McKinsey & Company, to support them in interpreting their data.[29]

Once the data have been interpreted and hypotheses are formed, the collaborative can then focus on finding solutions to the defined problems. Solution finding in the Itasca Project takes on two different forms. The task force will develop and recommend solutions to other organizations to test, or Itasca itself will incubate a solution and then spin it off. Often, Itasca will maintain a connection with this spun-off work, even if it is being carried out in other organizations.

With solutions developed, you then must reflect on progress. *Analyzing and reflecting* is the process of determining if the solutions are effective and learning from them to gain a better understanding of the problem and the solutions that are needed to achieve results. In the case of the Itasca Project, Barmann says:

> We do a little bit of [analyzing and reflecting] at the task force level. I like to sit down with the task force chairs and do that. And we have the Working Team, which is the group that meets every Friday morning. I think they are the ones that drive this in a big way because it sometimes takes some time to do this analyzing and reflecting. We keep the task forces that we want on our agenda as time goes on. [In those meetings, we talk about] how the Task Forces are doing, what their impact has been. And ask are there connections that still need to be made? Are there barriers that need to be removed? I think having the structure of the ongoing Working Team really enables that.

Committing to this kind of learning orientation as a collaborative is harder than it sounds. More likely than not, partners were invited to participate because of their expertise. They have been rewarded and promoted throughout their professional career because of their experience. And now they're being asked to sit in a room in front of each other and expose all the things they do wrong every day and don't know how to fix. This is not a behavior that feels natural for most people, and it involves a level of risk and vulnerability most have not been expected to exhibit daily.

This is a muscle that can be built over time, however, so it's important to invest in periods of reflection and opportunities to build trust within the cross-sector partnerships. This means that not investing the time or failing to make room for what seem like "touchy-feely," nice-to-have-but-not-necessary conversations can negatively impact what a group can accomplish and how quickly.

Even though it has its challenges, moving from this cycle of "problem defining" to "analyzing and reflecting" is one of the best investments you can make in your collaborative. A city that's had success tackling one problem using collective, data-based problem solving is far more likely to take on another challenge. And when that city is able to create a lasting impact on a variety of issues, other cities will notice and be open to trying the same approach themselves. It becomes a positive, health-producing virus that spreads and spreads, from community to community.

The Working Cities Challenge (WCC) demonstrates how a cultural virus like this can be a powerful instrument of change. WCC started out as an initiative led by the Federal Reserve Bank of Boston modeled from the efforts of Living Cities through the Integration Initiative (described more fully in chapter 4) to advance collaborative leadership and support ambitious work to improve the lives of low-income people in smaller Massachusetts cities. Each city worked on a different issue, from health to entrepreneurship, but they *all* were committed to collective problem solving. Their efforts impressed state government and helped to change policy at the state level.

Through the WCC, collective problem solving spread not only between cities but also to the state level. Because of its connection to the Federal Reserve, the WCC has the power to "infect" other states and regions with the ability to create change. The initiative has expanded now to Rhode Island and will soon expand into Connecticut, in part supported by Living Cities. We are currently in talks with other Federal Reserve banks across the country, so as you read this, the WCC may have positively infected many more places to date.

CHOOSE AN APPROACH FOR CONTINUOUS IMPROVEMENT

An important part of keeping results on course is making sure everyone gets together regularly to reassess what's working and what's not working—and why. Which strategies have pushed us closer to our goals? Which ones have turned out be failures? How can we make sure we prevent similar failures in the future?

I've noticed, though, that people like to come at the process of determining strategies the other way around: they already have a strategy in motion that they've invested time and money in, so now they want to make that strategy works. They squeeze it and push it and stretch it, trying to get it to be an effective way of reaching their goal—instead of looking at the goal first and then replacing the strategy if necessary, if it's not the right one to get them where they want to go.

All of us get attached to the familiar strategies we've been using for a while; that's just a natural human tendency. When we have our focus on data (in other words, measurable results), however, rather than any single strategy, it's easier to let go of strategies that turn out not to be as effective. Without that focus on data, it's easy to just keep doing what we've always done, without ever realizing that what we're doing may not actually be the best approach. On the other hand, when accountability is "baked into" an ongoing problem-solving process, it's an engine that keeps driving your partnership toward its shared result.

There are many ways to keep your partnership on track with what's working. Here I'll describe two that we've used: A3 problem solving and Results-Based Accountability (RBA).

A3 PROBLEM SOLVING

One of the problem-solving tools we use was created in the business world: A3, a structured continuous-improvement approach that was first used by the Toyota Corporation. The name "A3" comes from the fact that the structure is simple enough that it will fit on a single sheet of A3 paper.

The process is just one approach to continuously improving your partnership's work. It helps you fully leverage the data-driven feedback loop mentioned in chapter 3. The A3 is based on PDSA framework: plan, do, study, act. It's a simple iterative process where you plan for the work you want to do, execute on that plan, collect data and reflect on what happened, and then act to make changes to your original plan.

One of our collaborative initiatives, the Prepare Learning Circle, used the A3 to support their work to get low-income people into jobs with self-sustaining wages. They created an A3 on various strategies, such as an educational campaign for a training program or an initiative to engage employers, and tested out various ways to effectively deliver those strategies. The A3 tool helped the members of the Prepare Learning Circle to set a timeline for action and be specific about who does what by when. This specificity helped increase accountability among partners.

Tools

StriveTogether
Every Child. Cradle to Career.

A3 Reporting Tool   **Strengthening Pathways to Construction and Manufacturing - All Hands Raised**   2/25/15

Result | Plan

Result Statement: Multnomah County youth have the support and clear pathways they need to enter career training in construction and manufacturing.

Core Indicator: Number of students graduating from high school and moving on to post-secondary career training through supported pathways into construction and manufacturing.

Measurement Tool: Oregon Dept. of Education for graduation data, multiple sources for entry into career training including pre-apprenticeship programs, individual employers, and community colleges (no single comprehensive source identified)

Current Conditions/Baselines | Plan

EXAMPLE OF PROGRAM-LEVEL DATA CURRENTLY COLLECTED BY ONE MANUFACTURING-FOCUSED PARTNER PROGRAM

Total number of program graduates: '38
Total number of surveys completed (collected data through online surveys): 25
Number employed in MFG: 11 (44%) (7 receive full benefits)
Number employed in Non-MFG: 3 (none receive benefits)
Number enrolled in post-secondary: 6 (5 in MFG or ENG field, one employed at MFG and taking MFG courses)
Number in military: 3
Number doing nothing: 2

Graduates in MFG or Skilled Trades make $3.88 more per hour than graduates employed on non-MFG or skilled trades.
Graduates in MFG are more likely to receive full benefits and receive overtime.

- 5-yr cohort grad rate for CTE completers*
- Overall 5-year cohort grad rate

Total	69% / 90%
American Indian / ...	39% / 75%
Asian / Pacific Islander	79% / 96%
Black / African American	58% / 88%
Hispanic / Latino	61% / 87%
Multiracial	67% / 84%
White	73% / 91%

Manufacturing
16% Growth
15,000 New Jobs

Construction
27% Growth
15,000 New Jobs

Targets(s) | Plan

GLOBAL AIM (3-5 years): By 2019, X% of Multnomah County high school graduates enroll in post-secondary education or career training within sixteen months and an increased percentage persist through their first year, with disparities impacting students of color narrowing in both enrollment and persistence.

SMART AIM (1 year): By 2018, increase the number of students graduating from high school and moving on to post-secondary career training through supported pathways into construction and manufacturing from X to Y. (Baseline needed; target and approximately 5 percentage point increase)

Factor Analysis (Story Behind the Baselines) | Plan

- In order to access these pathways students need information, encouragement and concrete guidance on next steps
- Educators typically do not have direct personal experience with trades/manufacturing pathways
- Direct personal relationships are often the key factor in connecting young people to these pathways
- There is a "break in the chain" between high school and entry into skilled trades/manufacturing due to systemic barriers, lack of awareness and stigma – as such young people often incur college debt or pursue lower-wage jobs after high school and take several years before entering trades/manufacturing training pathways.

Interventions/Strategies | Do

Intervention One: Educate educators about construction & manufacturing career paths (immersion experiences and materials/ tools)

Intervention Two: Leverage successful education industry partnerships to identify and scale the practices that help students transition into construction & manufacturing careers

Action Plan (Who, What, When, Where & How) | Do

Strategy One
- Develop useful/engaging tools/visuals to portray these career pathway and inspire action and awareness among educators
- Plan and implement Industry for A Day event to provide an immersion in the construction and manufacturing pathways for high school counselors, principals, district leaders and school board members.
- Identify specific options for follow-up action commitments from those participating in Industry for A Day
- Partner with Worksystems, Inc. to plan and promote a 3-day "externship" for high school educators in the summer

Strategy Two
- Launch a Collaborative of programs focused on supporting high school students into construction and manufacturing pathways
- Affirm goals and measures and collect data from all participating programs
- Implement multiple PDSA cycles to test and identify effective practices in supporting students into these pathways
- Share/scale effective practices

Status | Study
To be completed based on progress.

Action Commitments | Act
To be completed based on progress.

A sample A3 tool from our partners All Hands Raised, in Portland, OR.

Download this tool at http://tools.changeforimpact.org

THE RESULTS-BASED ACCOUNTABILITY (RBA) APPROACH

At Living Cities, we found that the Results-Based Accountability (RBA) framework, championed by Mark Friedman as well as the Annie E. Casey Foundation, is a useful tool to help social-sector collaborations better align their work through a process of identifying a shared result, and then developing outcomes and shorter-term measures that link programs to this overall shared result. We used this framework to help our partners set up their data-driven feedback loops, which I talked about in chapter 3.

We've identified several important elements of this extremely useful "tool set." If you are interested in learning more about, I encourage you to pick up *Trying Hard Is Not Good Enough* by Mark Friedman.

Identify Your "Customers" and Define Performance Measures Accordingly

The RBA process pushes organizations to articulate the role they play in community-wide impact by identifying specific "customers"— the people who benefit from their services. This might seem like common sense, but the questions that the framework poses as part of this process to determine whether customers are better off are elegant and powerful in their simplicity:

- How much did we do?

- How well did we do it?

- Is anyone better off?

Of course, the last question is the most important, but asking all three of the questions helps to identify where there might be disconnects between effort and results.

At Living Cities, we are constantly asking ourselves how issues that impact the lives of low-income people are interrelated. For example, we know that connecting people to jobs is about more than job-training programs (though job-training programs are certainly important). In order to bridge the opportunity gaps we encounter, we must also look at an entire range of variables, including things such as cradle-to-career educational systems, transit, access to technology, and policies around hiring people with criminal records. At the same time we cast a wide net when it comes to looking at the factors that contribute to a specific problem, we must also be very focused and clear about which results we will hold ourselves accountable for.

You'll note in the example from chapter 3 where we changed how your organization works, we separated the performance measures we were using into six-to-ten-year and three-to-six-year cycles and key drivers. We as Living Cities decided to do this because our communities were challenged by the leap from overwhelming, longer-term change to manageable, shorter-term change. One of the few tweaks we provided to RBA was highlighting the journey from programmatic level change to systems change.

Disaggregate Data

Because you need to know who your "customers" are, separating the outcome data you collect into categories such as race, ethnicity, income level, and gender has vital importance for any effort that seeks community-wide impact. People sometimes think that it sounds more inclusive—and will trigger less controversy—if they articulate goals as results that bring benefits to *all*. Actually, however, generic, population-wide results are often too vague to be meaningful. They don't allow communities to really hone in on who is being left behind—and they don't tell cross-sector partnerships where concentrated efforts can have the greatest impact.

This type of segmentation may be challenging for your partners or you. We've learned from work in communities around the country that looking at data on segmented groups such as African American men or Latina girls can bring up some hard conversations. But if you're reticent about segmentation because of a desire for inclusivity, think about what other types of organizations do. Companies who sell your favorite soaps, clothes, and cars use disaggregated data to craft their messaging to ensure that you buy their products. Political candidates use this data to ensure that you vote for them. So why wouldn't you use this data to help you craft solutions that address our most important problems?

The Living Cities mission of working with cross-sector leaders in cities to build a new type of urban practice aimed at dramatically improving the economic well-being of low-income people requires that we understand how race, place, class, and other factors affect access to opportunity. We've learned that "one size fits all" is not a good enough approach. To get at supporting the "all," you must also look at the components that make up the "all."

Understand the Story Behind the Data

As we discussed in chapter 1, Donella Meadows encouraged people to shift focus away from a problem's symptoms and looked instead at the root causes of the problem. The RBA process builds on this research and pushes folks to dig deep to identify the "roots" revealed in the data. It is not enough to ask ourselves "why?" once, find a fast answer, and then move on. Instead, we must keep asking ourselves the same question in the same way that a doctor would investigate the causes of symptoms of a chronic disease before making a diagnosis and prescribing treatment.

When we forget to keep asking "why?" we often end up wasting our efforts on strategies that don't actually do what we want them to do, because they fail to consider all the contributing factors. For example, in the course of developing the Integration Initiative, the Living Cities team, led by Robin Hacke and Marian Urquilla, was repeatedly struck by gaps in what we have come to refer to as "capital absorption capacity"—the ability of communities to make effective use of different forms of capital to support the needs of underserved communities. We thought that finding the capital would be enough. Instead, we discovered that we needed to build an ongoing practice around understanding the story behind the data. When we did that, we could design better strategies from the outset.

THE OPEN-SOURCING CHANGE TOOL SET

One of the other strategies that Living Cities uses to create lasting impact is what we call "open-sourcing social change." This means that we freely share everything we've learned so that others can try out the things that we are learning and that our partners are learning so we can all benefit. As we work with leaders across the country, we are seeing that there's a real hunger out there for innovative approaches to social change that transcend sector, locale, and issue. In response, we are:

- making our learning open and accessible to others in real time

- engaging others in ways that allow us to learn from their work

- intentionally weaving networks of thought leaders, practitioners, and innovators to foster deeper collaboration and cocreation of solutions

- producing, curating, and sharing stories, content, tools, and resources that inspire change and fill unmet needs in the field

Open-source, real-time knowledge sharing is central to everything we do. What's more, we believe it is a key contributor to the changes we want to see in the world. We are committed to working with others to make this practice course-of-business in the social change field because we believe it's another tool that makes a lasting impact possible. When we share what we are learning, others can "leapfrog" our work and achieve their results faster.

The approach to open-sourcing social change challenges the bias that knowledge is only worth sharing after the work is complete and "proven." Instead, we believe that today's leaders can benefit from information shared during all stages of development, from an early hunch or idea to an emerging approach that requires additional testing. Social media technologies—from Twitter to the blogosphere—offer new opportunities to make connections and expand impact.

Our CEO, Ben Hecht, frequently talks about "knowledge as a social good." This idea is baked into the core of Living Cities' operations—we believe that it is our obligation to share what we are learning with our partners in the field. If we hold everything we've learned close to the chest, then we doom others to repeat the same mistakes we've made. By continuously sharing what we've seen from our work, we help others get dramatically better and faster results for the people they serve. It also helps us better achieve our own organizational outcomes.

We decided to intentionally open-source social change when our partners around the country repeatedly asked us for more support on engaging community members. Around this same time, many other leaders across the country were speaking out that the collective impact model we were using to create lasting impact was too "top down" and needed more integrated involvement from community representatives. In response, we created a community engagement e-course, which taught us four key lessons:

1. Be Responsive and Targeted

Because of our unique position supporting more than seventy collective impact initiatives across the country, we decided to *respond* to these requests for more information and figure out how collective impact initiatives could better engage with communities.

We began our exploration with two *targeted* approaches. We convened our partners to explore the topic, hosting a daylong event that brought together experts from across the country to discuss the topic, bringing to the surface relevant tools and resources. We also worked with a subset of our members to collect examples from their work on how to best engage with communities for large-scale change initiatives.

2. Start Broad and Go Narrow

The convening and work with our members resulted in a wealth of information about collective impact. The research, perspectives, and examples we collected were so *broad* they could have filled a book. But our goal with this exploration wasn't to be comprehensive—it was to respond to a need and offer resources that help people do their work better.

So instead of publishing an expansive research paper on community engagement and collective impact, we decided to *narrow down* the scope of our work and create a resource that was actionable and easily digestible. We developed an e-course that featured several modules on the topics that we felt were most relevant to practitioners. Our assumption was that people did not have the time to comb through pages and pages of resources that a typical white paper might provide, and so we made sure the e-course clearly directed people to resources we felt were most relevant for the challenges they were facing.

Once we decided we wanted to develop an e-course, we went back out to the people involved in our initial exploration of the topic to double-check our thinking on which resources practitioners needed to do their work better. We also spoke with other leaders in the field who we thought could help us improve the e-course based on their experiences. And then we offered the course for free.

3. Continuously Learn to Increase Impact

The e-course turned out to be a huge success. We had more than a thousand people sign up within the first couple of weeks. Even though the e-course was initially successful, though, we didn't call it a day. We collected data throughout the e-course to make sure we were meeting participants' needs.

This focus on data had one goal in mind: behavior change. If people signed up for this e-course but didn't end up changing their behavior, then we would not have achieved success. The goal of the e-course, and all Living Cities' open-sourcing social change work, is to ensure that positive behavior change is happening all over.

The initial results from the e-course are encouraging, but behavior change at the field level is hard to measure and track. We're *continuously learning* how to better understand our *impact*—and *increase* it. Based on surveys, on average participants indicated that the e-course changed the way they think about community engagement and collective impact and that the materials were applicable to their work. These are proxies for behavior change, but at least they're proxies that point in the right direction.

4. Repurpose Content to Impact Different Audiences

We can reuse the work we did for the e-course, *repurposing the content* by presenting it in new ways, such as on a Tamarack Institute webinar and at a Grantmakers for Effective Organizations conference. Most recently our work on community engagement and collective impact was included in the *Community Development* review, allowing us to *impact different audiences* (in this case, academics and university professionals).

After we launched the e-course, the information we offered triggered changes in ways we hadn't foreseen. Like the Working Cities Challenge in Massachusetts, this was another example of an infectious "virus" spreading all by itself, creating a lasting impact. Based on the e-course's content, the United Way of New York City restructured their department to better address the issues of community engagement. The United Way of New York City isn't formally connected with Living Cities in any way, and yet because of our open-source policy, we were able to help them improve themselves.

Another example is Feeding America. Feeding America has a mission quite different from many of our partners—one that's focused on how to increase food security for people through its network of food banks rather than on education and economic development. Because of our open-source sharing, however, they are applying lessons we'd learned from other groups—and are using them to accelerate their results. And we hope to learn from their experiences and share them with others as well.

Living Cities has become a platform that attracts more information, which we can in turn pass along, thus creating more knowledge, which in turn translates to more influence and greater impact. The lessons we learn today will help to shape the work being done tomorrow, not only by ourselves but also by many other people and agencies. We contribute to creating a new culture of possibility and change.

The change virus will keep spreading indefinitely, because people are dynamic. They don't stay in one place. As they get promoted or move to new networks, they bring their information and knowledge with them. They start to use the information in new ways in their new settings. Other people learn from them. It's a cycle that never stops.

I came of age as a professional in General Electric at an amazing inflection point of outcomes and technology. And while I've always been committed to social change regardless of which industry was responsible for my paycheck, I have always been struck by the fact that the social sector is often not aspiring to achieve measurable outcomes at a rapid pace like the private sector. Similarly, the private sector often does not understand or invest the capacities required to rapidly drive social change at scale. Clearly, no single leader, organization, or sector can have a lasting impact on the world's problems all by themselves. Complex, interconnected problems require interconnected solutions.

Open-source, real-time knowledge sharing is central to everything we do at Living Cities. It's a key contributor to the impact we want to have on the world. We are committed to working with others to make this practice course-of-business, so that all cross-sector partnerships can become more powerful than ever before.

🎤 *Share Your Story*

What have you learned that can benefit another community? Visit **www.changeforimpact.org** to tell us how you used this book to create lasting impact and Living Cities may highlight your work.

BERMUDA TRIANGLE OF CROSS-SECTOR PARTNERSHIPS

We've learned a lot about what works and doesn't work when it comes to collaborating for change. No matter how much we know about building successful cross-sector partnerships, though, we've discovered that these partnerships all have a tendency to get caught in what we sometimes call the "Bermuda Triangle of Cross-Sector Partnerships." They flounder in this Bermuda Triangle, sometimes never to be seen again. The triangle looks like this:

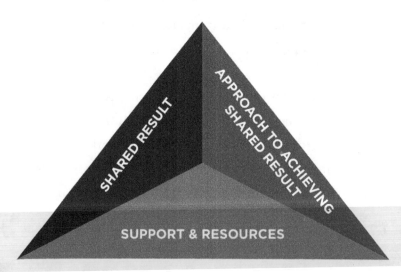

Whenever we see a cross-sector partnership unable to move forward, we suspect that it may be trapped in this treacherous triangle. There is hope, though! Partnerships can escape each of the three traps within the Bermuda Triangle.

The Shared Result Trap

As I described in chapter 3, organizations within cross-sector partnerships need to commit to shared results, and these need to be SMART (specific, measurable, actionable, relevant, and time-bound). "Ninety percent of the labor force of Chicago will be employed by 2020" is an example of a SMART goal. It allows the partnership to measure its progress toward achieving the shared result over time. But if a partnership has not agreed to a SMART shared result, then the partnership can find it difficult to communicate to potential partners the specific goals of the initiative and how they could help achieve those goals. A SMART shared result also helps a partnership track progress over time—without it, it can be difficult for a partnership to know if it's achieving what it set out to do. (To learn more about how to create a good shared result, flip back to chapter 3.)

Whenever a cross-sector partnership fails to be effective or move forward, reexamining the "shared-results" side of the triangle can be a useful step toward getting unstuck.

Support and Resources Trap

Getting people bought into an initiative and contributing their time is the first step to fully resourcing the partnership. The next step will be to secure financial commitments, which can come from the partners themselves or from other local or national funders. The obvious challenge at this end of the Bermuda Triangle is securing financial commitments, a challenge for any social-sector initiative. If you've already secured funding, you may be facing another challenge in this corner of the triangle: funding is running out or your partners have become fatigued in their involvement with your partnership and want to exit. This can happen several years into the work and is another way cross-sector partnerships start to flounder.

But this challenge can also be an opportunity. For a cross-sector partnership's work to have lasting impact, it must be sustainable even after the partnership itself stops its activities. To achieve this, members must consider how their work or portions of their work can be embedded in another institution. Often, this institution is a government agency, but it can be a regional planning body, a business or business partnership, a large nonprofit, or another type of local organization. Remember, the larger goal is more important than any partnership's private interests or reputation. If your goal is to increase job opportunities in your cities, and that goal is continuing to be achieved, then it doesn't matter if the work is being carried forward in another way by another organization. To learn more about how to resource your collaboration, check out chapter 6.

Approach to Achieving Shared Result Trap

The final side of the Bermuda Triangle can be the most harrowing. In our experience with cross-sector partnerships, we've found that partnerships can approach their work in three different ways:

1. They can focus on delivering projects and/or programs that provide services to individuals, such as housing support, after-school tutoring, or anything that directly benefits individual people.

2. They can work with senior leadership in organizations to change their behavior as it relates to the cross-sector partnership's purpose, including policy changes.

3.   They can do both these things.

If a partnership fits into the first category of primarily focusing on project and programs, it is at risk of paying too much attention to short-term solutions and not considering the root causes of the problems it's attempting to solve. If a partnership fits into the second category, it can be too focused on long-term, seemingly intangible solutions to large problems that people struggle to fully understand. A program/project cross-sector partnership could be doing a lot of work day-to-day delivering services but not be doing anything to ensure that its work will endure even if the partnership closed its doors. A partnership focused on longer-term changes could be working hard to have people buy in to its agenda, without any tangible results to secure the support of potential partners. To get out of this trap, cross-sector partnerships require both components embedded into their approach.

When cross-sector partners are caught in that last trap of the triangle, it can lead to conflict and tension. Addressing the issue is essential; otherwise conflict can limit or hinder the lasting impact partners are hoping to achieve. A certain degree of tension is inherent when any groups of people work together, however—and handled properly, tensions and conflict can actually contribute to your ultimate success.

 *Tools*

CROSS-SECTOR PARTNERSHIP ASSESSMENT

Many of the lessons presented in this book were used to create Living Cities' Cross-Sector Partnership Assessment, which is a free, 10 minute survey. The Assessment helps those engaged in cross-sector partnerships think through the development and progress of their partnership and provides immediate, tailored feedback, tools and resources to help partners get better results, faster. You can take the Assessment by visiting http://tools.changeforimpact.org.

Download this tool at http://tools.changeforimpact.org

YOU MAY BE UNIQUE, BUT YOU'RE NOT SPECIAL

Sometimes when we share our stories with fellow travelers, the first thing that comes to mind is all the ways our efforts are different from theirs: "They're focusing on African Americans, while our population is Latino"; "If we had a strong tech sector like they do, maybe we'd focus on small-business growth, but we don't"; or "Their economy is experiencing growth while ours is contracting, so their experience doesn't apply."

Of course, as we know from experience, no one has ever been able to lift a strategy wholesale from one community and plop it down into another. However, if you listen to the advice and wisdom offered within your network, you might realize that, while your community is unique, it may not be special. Perhaps some elements of RBA may be more helpful to you than the Bermuda Triangle of Cross-Sector Partnerships. Or maybe you can use the A3 tool if you tweak it just a little bit. Regardless of what you're facing, someone, somewhere has confronted that issue, and you can learn a great deal from what worked and what didn't, even if it is not a one-for-one match.

The tools I've described in this chapter are all ones Living Cities has used and refined many, many times. We know their worth. At the same time, we know that no tool can accomplish everything all by itself and that each must be applied based on the unique circumstances of your community. As we work together to close our world's opportunity gaps, we need to use as many tools as possible and put to use all the resources that are available.

With so many big challenges in the world today—and limited amounts of talent, time, and money—collaborative partnerships must use these resources to create a lasting impact, to become as effective as they can possibly be. Achieving this requires that partnerships not only change the way they collaborate; they must also change the way in which they find the resources to do their work.

Looking Forward: Change How Your Collaborative Does Its Work

Questions to consider:

- Do you think of your work in terms of programs or solutions to be tested?

- How have you invested in collective problem solving for your partners?

- Would the A3 tool or RBA framework be useful for your work?

- How can you better share your lessons learned with others?

- Is your collaborative struggling in these three areas?
    - defining a shared result
    - establishing resources and support
    - determining what approach to take to achieve a shared result

CHAPTER 6

CHANGE HOW YOU RESOURCE YOUR COLLABORATION

Wilson Boulevard in Northern Virginia is not a particularly remarkable place. It's a long concrete stretch lined intermittently with nondescript office buildings, Starbucks, and fast-food stops. But I love this street because it's where I had my first baby.

I'm not referring to my handsome son, Dylan; I'm referring to my other baby, my first real achievement in bridging the opportunity gaps I see in the world. As executive director of Year Up National Capital Region, I spent close to a decade raising and nurturing something from inception in a way I had never done before.

As I drove up Wilson Boulevard more than seven years after our doors opened, I thought about how much had changed during my time there. When I started Year Up National Capital Region, we had no corporate partners and were literally recruiting our students from behind fryolators. Seven years later, we had served more than a thousand young people, raised $20 million, hosted President Barack Obama, and continued to see more than 85 percent of our alumni in technical careers and higher education. I was one proud momma. Who wouldn't be?

So why, as I neared our building that one morning, did such a strange feeling come over me? It was something I had never felt before. I stopped my car and looked up at the windows to the second floor. We had new hills to climb, more young people to serve, and more important work to do. And then the unshakable reality hit me: I was not the one to take us there. I kept driving.

I had been blessed to find a platform that allowed me to leverage my passions and proficiencies to create a lasting impact. If it was time for me to move on, where could I go that would take me even further? Where could I work to close even more opportunity gaps? Prior jobs had pushed me to learn and grow, but with Year Up I had crossed a threshold from which there was no return. I had found work that was not only stimulating and challenging but also had meaning and reflected my personal values. I knew there'd be no going back.

Instead of thinking about where I wanted to work next, I started reflecting on what I wanted out of my next environment. The work to which I was most often drawn and the successful systems I'd most often built revolved around shepherding, stewarding, and investing in people. I genuinely wanted to help people be the best versions of themselves they could be. The thought of doing that in a new way and in a new environment was at once exhilarating and daunting.

The professional world, however, seemed to offer a limited number of options. At one end were jobs that provided both financial security and upward mobility. The people I'd encountered who had made these career choices took pride in their accomplishments, but many also saw their work as having come through personal trade-offs. Sometimes they felt empty, often they felt regretful, and almost always they were seeking greater meaning than their lives currently offered them. On the other end, people whose work was focused on social justice or community activism felt they had meaning up the wazoo. And contrary to an often-unsaid assumption, these were folks who felt accomplished and proud of their achievements; they weren't envious of those on the other end of the spectrum. What they did lament, however, was that their commitment to service and mission didn't always pay the bills. In fact, it often imposed limitations on the opportunities, education, and quality of life they could provide for their loved ones. So these were my two choices? Wealth or meaning, take your pick!

But I wanted both. I wanted professional accomplishment but not at the expense of meaning. I wanted meaning but not at the expense of my family's well-being. I wanted to pursue my purpose while being true to my values. And by the looks of it, I wasn't alone in wanting these things. So I set out on a journey to build just that.

A model began to form in my head, one with which I believed could set in motion a cycle of perpetual motivation, purpose, and success.

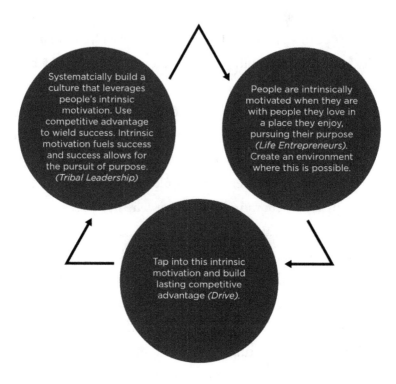

I became convinced that if there was an organization wherein people could always live, learn, and grow, then success would follow. We would be intentionally grooming and developing people in pursuit of their purpose. And when people's passions and purpose are nurtured, they do their best work. Think about the difference in output when you're doing something you're passionate about versus something you feel obligated to do!

This might sound a bit pie-in-the-sky but repeatedly, values-driven entrepreneurs are proving that my model can really work. These businesspeople focus on corporate culture not as a means to an end but as the actual end itself. Take Tony Hsieh, Zappos's CEO. His first and only priority was to focus on culture and customer service. The thinking was that if the employees were happy and the customers were happy, then the rest would fall into place. The result? Enthusiastic, devoted employees, loyal customers, and over $1 billion in gross merchandise sales.

LIVING CITIES' APPROACH TO RESOURCING COLLABORATION

At Living Cities, I found a place where people could believe that the pace and scale that was necessary was possible. This was in large part due to the members and other partners that fueled our efforts.

Living Cities was a place that was pulling together intrinsic motivations for "doing good" with practical financial principles. When I started working there, I helped others understand that both sides of this equation are necessary—that people must combine the resources of intrinsic motivation with financial resources to create lasting impact.

Closing the opportunity gaps—decreasing unemployment, fighting poverty, expanding educational and medical access—improves individuals' lives at the very same time that it also builds a stronger, healthier economy. In reality, the two sides aren't separate; they're just two faces to the same reality. They feed into each other. When we treat them as though they're separate, we limit what we can do in both areas.

At the same time, we want to make sure we're funding what really works. Even with so many dollars, so many plans, and so many committed people, the outcomes often still don't measure up to the goals. For example, despite numerous programs to help students learn better, schools continue to have low standardized test scores and high dropout rates. Unemployment is still a big problem in our nation, even though there are countless programs working to help people get jobs. Obesity numbers are still growing, despite all the health initiatives directed at fighting obesity.

One of the problems is this: dollars from various sources (whether financial institution lending or philanthropy grants or government agency funding) have landed on various programs in a fragmented, rather than unified, way. Ideally, all that money was meant to bring about the same goals, but because it was focused on programs instead of results, the funds often don't accomplish what they were meant to do.

To help you think about resourcing your collaborative work otherwise, this chapter will give you some different examples: aligning funding streams, working with diverse investors, impact investing, Pay for Success, and values-driven entrepreneurship.

ALIGN FUNDING STREAMS

In January 2014, Living Cities joined with the Commonwealth of Massachusetts, Goldman Sachs, Kresge, New Profit Foundation, and other local and national private and philanthropic funders to do something amazing. Together, they launched a seven-year, $27 million deal focusing on reducing recidivism and increasing employment for at-risk, formerly incarcerated young men in the Boston, Chelsea, and Springfield areas. The Massachusetts Juvenile Justice Social Innovation Financing Project, with Roca Inc., a Chelsea nonprofit, is designed to improve outcomes for hundreds of at-risk young men who are in the probation system or are leaving the juvenile justice system. Almost a thousand young men from Boston, Chelsea, and Springfield will be offered counseling, life skills, vocational training, and transactional employment to change their behavior and avoid violence.

At Living Cities, we've learned that there are far more funding options than just federal and private grants! We look beyond grants to focus on blending all types of capital to get faster, greater, and longer-lasting outcomes for low-income people. The Results-Based Accountability framework (described in chapter 5) feeds directly into this because it allows us to align funds with what really works.

The concept of effectively aligning funding streams is essential to what we do here at Living Cities. We work to make sure that funding lands in the right places so that it can contribute as powerfully as possible to positive change. Focusing on alignment allows us to articulate the conditions needed to bridge the gap between short- and long-term goals. We work to truly harness the power of many resources, leaders, programs, and systems to effectively bring about real and lasting change.

SEEK OUT DIVERSE INVESTORS

Everything we do at Living Cities is fueled by innovation. We are constantly trying to break the old eyeglasses we've been using to look at the world, so that we can gain fresh perspectives that will lead to new ideas. We bring the same approach to resourcing our work, expanding our pool of investors beyond the "usual suspects." We created the Blended Catalyst Fund, which blends grants, philanthropic debt, and commercial lending from ten different investors in order to fund promising initiatives that are working to have a lasting and powerful impact on our cities' problems.

The fact that our investors are both foundations and financial institutions is exciting, but it also means they each come to us with different sets of goals and limitations. This means we had to overcome some challenges to make the alignment of funding work. The challenges were similar to those faced by many organizations leading a cross-sector partnership. The experience of raising the Blended Catalyst Fund taught us four key practices for bringing together funders from different sectors. These four lessons were outlined by my colleagues at Living Cities, Director of Capital Innovation Eileen Neely, and Senior Associate Brian Nagendra, in a recent blog post.[30]

Be clear about the "why."

What are you hoping to do collectively that participants can't do on their own? In our case, we assumed that because of our investors' involvement in Living Cities, they would already know our why. Assuming always gets you in trouble! We had to clearly articulate what we wanted to do together before our investors fully bought into the idea of a new fund.

We learned that you *never* really reach a point where you can stop answering "why." The why is the shared end-game that we all want to achieve, so articulating it is the most crucial component to getting everyone on the same page, and it's also the key to keeping all of participants engaged. When we bring potential investments for the Blended Catalyst Fund to our investors now, we are purposeful about emphasizing the impact and innovation, because that is our why.

Allow and expect your partners to articulate their own positions and concerns.

When we first started building our fund, we believed we had to be the main interpreters and speak for our investors. We were operating as a hub-and-spoke. Instead of acting as a network, we were having one-on-one conversations to understand individual investor concerns. As we saw two groups of investor interests emerging, we continued the individual relationships and acted as a messenger between the groups, negotiating with each party, controlling the conversation and what was happening. When we opened up the process and asked our investors to voice their own opinions and concerns, it not only helped to build trust within the group, but it also built our investors' trust in us.

After the change in our approach, we had valuable discussions with investors setting expectations for what each wanted out of the fund, discussing how much risk each was comfortable taking on, and pushing each other to stretch.

Problem-solve together.

Working as a cross-sector partnership built our ability to resolve issues in the open. We realized that we didn't need to have all the answers: as commercial lenders appreciated the mission-first viewpoint of our foundation lenders, and the foundations started to think like the commercial lenders, we saw solutions coming from our investors themselves.

Instill a sense of urgency.

While the backbone organization doesn't need to come up with all the solutions, it does need to carry the urgency and own the process. At Living Cities, we started seeing action when we set a closing date and set the tone by convening weekly calls with all of our investors.

Working collaboratively with our investors helped us get to a better end-result than we initially imagined. By changing our behavior, we were able to build a robust culture of collaboration that not only made raising the Blended Catalyst Fund a valuable learning experience for us, but has already led to the fund's success as we look to test innovative impact investing approaches.

LEVERAGE IMPACT INVESTMENTS

Impact investments are investments made into companies, organizations, and funds with the intention of generating social and environmental impact alongside a financial return.[31] The market for impact capital is currently at $60 billion and will likely grow even bigger.[32] This kind of investment doesn't rely on convincing all the world's financial institutions to become do-gooders. It's not about convincing a group of bank CEOs to hold hands and stand around singing "Kumbaya." Instead, it's an opportunity to connect economic opportunity with social-sector needs in a way that works for both sides of the equation.

Right now, demand (or the amount of money looking to be invested for impact) exceeds supply (or the number of investments or products available for investment). That is changing rapidly and will continue to change as more for-profit and nonprofit companies, organizations (including Living Cites), and funds develop more "products." Eventually, though, these kinds of investments could add still more force and energy to the work we do to cross the opportunity gaps. They won't replace the existing fund sources currently being applied to social change—but they'll expand them, making lives better for many more low-income people, improving the cities where they live in new ways, and fueling innovation that helps overcome obstacles now standing in the way of critical progress.

New methodologies have been emerging over the past few years that support this investment practice. People feel good about putting their money into things they care about. It taps into the intrinsic motivations described in chapter 3.

Living Cities CEO, Ben Hecht, outlined several examples of impact investing in one of his blog posts.[33]

- **Crowdfunding.** Locally crowdfunded, direct investments are already showing how they can help generate much-needed capital for community development projects and more. Washington, DC, startup Fundrise, for example, allows pools of local investors to back real estate projects in their own neighborhoods, with contributions big or small. It already has aggregated more than $30 million for local projects.

- **Loan dollars raised and dedicated to place.** Organizations such as the Calvert Foundation are making it easier for citizens to lend money in their own communities. Calvert's Ours to Own campaign is hoping to raise more than $30 million from citizens that will be invested into their respective communities. In each metro area, every day, Americans will be able to invest as little as $20 through Calvert Foundation's Community Investment Note on Vested.org. Their collective investments will be pooled to provide the loan capital to the lending partners.

- **Peer-to-peer lending.** Microfinance grants that enable loans to entrepreneurs and others have been perfected internationally by groups such as Kiva. We are already seeing that concept being imported into the US in a limited number of cities through Kiva Cities. Each Kiva City is a partnership of community groups, leaders, and microfinance organizations working together to fill the funding gap faced by many of our nation's small businesses owners. Through microlending, people can help to crowdfund loans to small businesses as they start up or expand, creating jobs and stronger local communities.

- **Locally raised venture capital.** FastCoExist highlighted[34] a firm that is on the road to mainstreaming Direct Public Offerings (DPOs)—"where companies can advertise freely and directly to the public and sign up an unlimited numbers of 'accredited' and 'unaccredited' investors (in other words, anyone)." They featured DPOs for a pickle company, restaurants, and a current offering with CERO, a recycling co-op in Boston. They've raised more than $5 million so far.

PAY FOR SUCCESS

Pay for Success is one of the most promising and powerful tools Living Cities found for aligning investment funding with data-driven results. It's an innovative financing structure that redirects public spending by encouraging innovation—and rewarding initiatives that really work. It has a simple premise: what works gets money, and what doesn't work, doesn't. Private-sector companies—such as Morgan Stanley, Merrill Lynch, Goldman Sachs, or JP Morgan Chase, for example—bring money to the table to solve problems that might not otherwise concern them. They're comfortable doing that because the public sector is promising that they'll only have to fund what works.

Living Cities' work with Cuyahoga County, OH, gave us another example of the effectiveness of this technique, though it turned out differently than we had expected. The county was concerned that when mothers were released from prison, they often failed to connect with their children, who then ended up in foster care far longer than would have been necessary. In order to comply with the Pay for Success requirements, the county needed to achieve the outcome they wanted: more mothers being reunited with their children after prison release.

To do this, the county had to look at the existing system. They had to ask, "What are some of the things that are driving mothers' failure to connect with their children?" They discovered that the processes within the criminal justice system and those within the foster care system weren't communicating with each other—and this was creating a knowledge gap for the mothers. The women didn't understand that once they were out of prison they didn't have to give up custody of their children. Fixing the problem meant changing the county's IT systems so that whenever a mother was released from prison, the foster care system would be "pinged." Social workers would then know to begin the process of reconnecting the woman with her children.

The county was so impressed with the results that, in the end, they didn't need to use the Pay for Success funds. The changes they made repaired a broken system—and now mothers and children would be automatically reconnected, again and again and again, each time a mother was released from prison.

In our eyes, this wasn't a Pay for Success deal that fell apart; it was lasting impact successfully achieved. The Pay for Success program had pointed the county in the right direction, and that's all that really mattered to those of us at Living Cities. The big goal is always, always more important than how we get there. Understanding that—and believing it—is an essential part of changing the way we think about change.

We've found that successful Pay for Success transactions depend on what Living Cities' Director of Capital Innovation Eileen Neely calls the 4 Ps of Pay for Success. She and Andy Rachlin of The Reinvestment Fund defined these 4 Ps in the following way:[35]

1. Partnership

With so many people necessary at the table in Pay for Success initiatives (government or other payers, investors, intermediaries, evaluators, and service providers), there's an enormous need for trust, collaboration, and agreement on a shared vision and metrics for success. The tighter the partnership and the more aligned the goals of the project, the more likely it is to succeed. When things go wrong (and they inevitably will!), a set of partners committed to a shared goal is critical to finding a way forward.

Partnership is hard to quantify, but it *can* be objectively assessed by asking the following questions:

- Do the partners instinctively frame work in shared terms?
- Can the partners clearly identify challenges they have faced in working together—and do their responses to those challenges suggest an ability to clearly communicate, put self-interest aside, and compromise to find a solution?
- Do the partners have strong interpersonal relationships?

The answers to these questions will help a cross-sector group assess how successful their partnership is.

2. Program

Ultimately, the repayment of the investment is dependent on the program's ability to deliver successful outcomes. To determine the likelihood that the program will deliver those outcomes, it's helpful to understand both the evidence-based research and the implementation aspects of the program. In other words, what does the research say about the type and effectiveness of the intervention? What factors contribute toward its successful implementation? What is the track record of the service provider in producing the outcomes? Pay for Success projects are unique because they require that people with financial expertise work alongside people with program expertise, in ways they may not be accustomed to doing.

3. Policy

Another aspect to consider when underwriting a Pay for Success investment is the capacity of the public sector (or other payer) to create a policy environment that supports the project. Whether it's passing a law to provide a mechanism to fund outcome payments or creating a reserve account within an existing budget line, having the payer's buy-in is critical to ensuring a commitment to the success payments, as well as to providing ongoing leadership of the project. If the payer is the public sector, as has been usually the case, having a government "champion" who spans political terms and can continue to provide leadership and oversight of the project is integral to the project's success.

4. Process

Not only does the program need to be sound, but it also must work within a process. When we talk about "process," we mean how the individuals in the project move through the system from beginning (usually referral) to end (ideally successful achievement of the desired outcome)—and every step along the way. Data must not only be collected but also efficiently passed along and shared, in order to prevent any gaps in information sharing or program delivery. Processes often break down at the intersection of different agencies or data systems, so it's important to understand how the approach will address coordination across bureaucratic lines. The more the process differs from business as usual, the more critical it is to assess the potential problem areas and identify solutions before they arise.

VALUES-DRIVEN ENTREPRENEURSHIP

Wealth or meaning? Comfort or fulfillment? As more people are leaving their respective posts at the far ends of the wealth-versus-meaning spectrum, they leave a larger and larger space to fill. Enter the values-driven entrepreneur.

Successful impact investments have fueled a new wave of entrepreneurs who are intentionally trying to contribute to solving social problems while building a successful, for-profit venture. The values-driven entrepreneur believes it doesn't have to be a choice. Not only can companies do well *and* do good, but they also do well *by* doing good. As our world becomes more complex, people's places of work occupy a greater space in their lives—and this means that work must be more than simply earning dollars; it must also help to meet people's need for meaning in their lives.

As a result, companies are not only impacting communities, but companies *are* the communities within which people exist. Whether it's Zappos or Timberland or Clif Bar, the leaders of these companies don't just adhere to a set of values they brainstormed in a boardroom. Their values serve as an inner compass; the values guide them and lead them down the path to purpose.

Unlike nonprofit ventures, these social entrepreneurs can (and do) attract early- and later-stage private capital from investors who expect a market rate return on their investment. When they get that return from the social-sector solutions they've helped to fund, it's another way to spread the "virus" we mentioned in chapter 5. The more businesses see this investment approach working, the more likely they will be to try it too.

Our work at Living Cities has attracted new players to help cross the opportunities gaps. Included in this list are Omidyar, which is focused on procurement and entrepreneurship in different ways for job creation; the Kauffman Foundation, which focuses on high-growth entrepreneurship; and the Markle Foundation, whose work centers on the intersection of jobs, job quality, and job growth. Once the focus is on sharing information and filling gaps, new folks come to the table. Our job at Living Cities is to offer a neutral platform where they can weave themselves together in a network of different approaches that will all drive change.

And for the values-driven entrepreneur, it isn't about walking this path alone. It's about leaving the path open for as many other people as possible so that they can find their own path to purpose, while at the same time working together to achieve something greater for the collective.

The Dallas Impact Investing Collaborative is an example of a network we launched locally so that its members could test and apply strategies—and ultimately learn from each other what works and what doesn't. Dallas has over $2 billion of foundation assets, and about 95 percent of it would have been invested in *something* anyway. It's not new money that we raised or pulled out of the community; it already existed. Now it can be used toward solving social problems in the community, while still earning a return. Meanwhile, the members of the Dallas Impact Investing Collaborative can learn more quickly because Living Cities has prioritized open-source learning over programs.

Is this way of doing business sustainable? Will it appeal to broader markets? Can it be scaled? Yes, yes, and yes! Proof of this comes when companies who take a values-driven approach consistently outperform the market no matter the industry, service, or product.

DOING GOOD AND DOING WELL

When I quit my position as executive director of Year Up National Capital Region, most people told me I was crazy to think I could do good (for society) *and* do well (financially). Those two things seemed incompatible. But I'd seen it happen. Furthermore, a wave of successful businesses was blossoming at the intersection of doing good and doing well, companies such as Tom's Shoes, Honest Tea, and Change.Org. While there was still skepticism, these soon-to-be influential social enterprises proved that aligning social and financial impact was both possible *and* profitable. I wasn't crazy after all.

I believe the next wave of businesses will do well *and* do good so the approach is a competitive advantage. As a result, the question at dinner parties will not be "what do you do?"—it will be "what problem do you solve?"

We still have a long way to go. But my hope is that we can keep the ripples of change constantly flowing wider and wider. We can actually change the way the world does business. And doing that will have a powerful and lasting impact. Together we can bridge the opportunity gaps.

Share Your Story

Have examples of doing well and doing good? Visit **www. changeforimpact.org** to share your story with others and Living Cities may highlight your work.

Looking Forward: Change How You Resource Your Collaboration

Questions to consider:

- How can you better align existing funding streams in your community?

- How can you leverage a diverse group of investors for additional resources?

- Could impact investing or Pay for Success be leveraged to support your collaborative?

- How are you working with values-driven entrepreneurs in your community to support your work?

CONCLUSION

I recently had a hankering for my Aunt Janice's legendary biscuits. Her biscuits are fluffy, buttery, light, and utterly delectable. So when I asked her for the recipe, I was delighted to discover that it had only four ingredients: flour, buttermilk, shortening, and butter. Simple, right? I bought the ingredients, mixed them up, and then baked a batch of biscuits. I could hardly wait for the oven timer to ring so that I could taste them.

But when I bit into one, I was totally disappointed. Even though I'd followed the recipe to the letter, my biscuits had turned out hard as rocks. I knew my sister had recently mastered Aunt Janice's recipe, so I called her up to ask what I'd done wrong.

My sister explained that while the recipe is straightforward and the ingredients are simple, mastering the process takes time. You have to commit to improving your biscuits each time you bake a batch—which means asking Aunt Janice questions along the way, while at the same time improving your technique based on what you find works best for you, in your own kitchen.

In many ways, driving social change requires a similar approach. Does every attempt at collaboration end up producing the effects we'd hoped for? Of course not. But ranting about the shortcomings of collaborative work is like yelling at the oven because of failed biscuits. We can get too focused on principles and theoretical frameworks when instead we should be encouraging and supporting a long-term commitment to continuous learning and improvement.

In this book, we've discussed many of the tools that work together to create a lasting impact. These may seem deceptively simple, but it is hard work to wield these tools effectively, and there is no manual in the world that will make that work easier. It's an endlessly complex task.

More important than the tools are the people who wield the tools and the result they are working to achieve. At Living Cities, we encourage leaders to apply the principles of lasting impact for one reason only: we believe the scale and scope of our nation's most pressing problems require cross-sector leaders to work together to solve them.

How can we compensate for the shortcomings of the tools we use? By being willing to:

- change how we think about change

- change how we create change

- change how our organizations work

- change how we collaborate

- change how our collaboratives do their work

- change how we resource our collaborations

These changes are built on creating communities of practice where leaders learn from and with each other on the path to social change. We close the opportunity gaps in our world when we commit ourselves to learning in public, open-sourcing social change, because when community leaders are vulnerable enough to share what is not working, they tap into the collective problem solving that makes change possible. We also achieve lasting impact when we have an ongoing commitment to continuous improvement. Each community must relentlessly ask itself what is working, what is not working, and why. Communities must diligently channel their resources toward what does work and abandon what does not.

This work is hard and takes diligence and care and feeding. And while I must be honest that I wasn't willing to put in the time to make better biscuits, I am committed to doing whatever it takes to improve the lives and opportunities of people across this country. So let's stop yelling at our ovens and start working together to achieve a lasting impact on our world.

Share Your Story

Visit **www.changeforimpact.org** to tell us how you used this book to create lasting impact and Living Cities may highlight your work.

ABOUT THE AUTHOR

Tynesia Boyea-Robinson exemplifies cross-sector leadership. In her current role as Chief Impact Officer at Living Cities, Tynesia works with cities across the country to ensure that investment leads to measurable impact. Tynesia's experience as an entrepreneur, Six Sigma blackbelt, and technologist uniquely positions her to catalyze a results-driven era of social change.

For example, through effective cross-sector partnerships, Tynesia helped establish the Social Innovation Fund and the Workforce Investment and Opportunity Act. As founding executive director of Year Up National Capital Region (NCR) and president and CEO of Reliance Methods, she demonstrated that business and community goals could powerfully align toward mutual outcomes. Under her leadership, Year Up NCR raised $20M, was recognized by President Obama, and continues to place thousands of low-income young adults in careers with family sustaining wages. Through Reliance Methods, she helps Fortune 500 clients like the Carlyle Group,

Marriott, and others source productive talent through unconventional practices. Earlier in her career, Tynesia was a leader within several business units at General Electric. From transforming the entire company to leverage technology for online sales to leading an international mortgage bank acquisition, her experience at GE groomed her to achieve outcomes regardless of industry.

Tynesia has been a featured speaker for a broad array of audiences including South by Southwest and the White House Council for Community Solutions. She has published several articles, which have been featured in the *Washington Post*, *Forbes* and in *Leap of Reason: Managing to Outcomes in an Era of Scarcity*. Her work was also highlighted in the *New York Times* bestseller *A Year Up* as well as in the Harvard Business School case study *Year Up: A Social Entrepreneur Builds High Performance*. She serves on numerous boards and committees, including for Duke University's Sanford School of Public Policy.

Tynesia received her MBA from Harvard Business School and has a dual degree in electrical engineering and computer science from Duke University. She and her college sweetheart, Keith, are committed to indoctrinating their children, Dylan and Sydney, with a love of Duke basketball and all things geeky and sci-fi.

ABOUT LIVING CITIES

For twenty-five years, Living Cities has harnessed the collective power of the world's largest foundations and financial institutions to develop and scale new approaches for creating opportunities for low-income people and improving the cities where they live. Its investments, research, networks, and convenings catalyze fresh thinking and combine support for innovative, local approaches with real-time sharing of learning to accelerate adoption in more places. Additional information can be found at www.livingcities.org.

ENDNOTES

1   Learn more about the work of Year Up on the Opportunity Divide at www.yearup.org/opportunity-divide/.

2   Rakesh Kochhar and Richard Fry, "Wealth Inequality Has Widened Along Racial, Ethnic Lines Since End of Great Recession," Pew Research Center, www.pewresearch.org/fact-tank/2014/12/12/racial-wealth-gaps-great-recession/.

3   Bureau of Labor Statistics, "Labor Force Statistics from the Current Population Survey," www.bls.gov/web/empsit/cpsee_e16.htm, accessed 9/16/16.

4   Michael Fletcher, "Study Ties Black-White Wealth Gap to Stubborn Disparities in Real Estate," *Washington Post*, www.washingtonpost.com/business/economy/study-ties-black-white-wealth-gap-to-stubborn-disparities-in-real-estate/2013/02/26/8b4b3f50-8035-11e2-b99e-6baf4ebe42df_story.html.

5   Jennifer Elias, "Venture Capital in Silicon Valley Isn't Diverse, And That's A Problem For America," Fast Company, www.fastcompany.com/3042887/diversity-in-tech-follow-the-money-vcs.

6   To go deeper into the theory behind systems change, see donellameadows.org.

7   Lawrence M. Fisher, "The Prophet of Unintended Consequences," *Strategy + Business,* Fall 2005, www.strategy-business.com/article/05308?gko=35c59.

8   Isaac Castillo, "First, Do No Harm . . . Then Do More Good," in *Leap of Reason: Managing to Outcome in an Era of Scarcity* (Venture Philanthropy Partners: Washington, DC, 2011), 95–98.

9   Natalie Angier, "Edward O. Wilson's New Take on Human Nature," *Smithsonian Magazine,* April 2012, www.smithsonianmag.com/science-nature/edward-o-wilsons-new-take-on-human-nature-160810520/#oy56SZAEpFUa3YIc.99.

10   For more check-in question ideas, visit www.livingcities.org/resources/305-meeting-icebreakers.

11   To learn more, read this Living Cities blog post by Theresa Gardella, February 17, 2015, www.livingcities.org/blog/776-community-engagement-s-inner-circle-making-investments-where-they-count.

12   Nexus, "Building the Field of Community Engagement," http://nexuscp.org/our-work/building-the-field-of-community-engagement/.

13   Ibid.

14   John Kania and Mark Kramer, "Collective Impact," *Stanford Social Innovation Review,* 2011.

15   Jeff Edmondson and Nancy L. Zimpher, *Striving Together: Early Lessons in Achieving Collective Impact in Education.*

16   Adrian Cho, "Gravitational Waves, Einstein's Ripples in Spacetime, Spotted for First Time," *Science,* Feb. 11, 2016, www. sciencemag.org/news/2016/02/gravitational-waves-einsteins-ripples-spacetime-spotted-first-time. Learn more about the cross-sector aspect of this discovery at the Intersector Project: http://intersector. com/what-can-the-discovery-of-gravitational-waves-teach-us-about-cross-sector-collaboration/.

17   Lynda Gratton, *The Key: How Corporations Succeed by Solving the World's Toughest Problems* (New York: HarperCollins, 2015).

18   E. Andrew Balas, " From Appropriate Care to Evidence-Based Medicine," *Pediatric Annals* 27:9 (September 1998), 581–584.

19   NPR Staff, "How TV Brought Gay People into Our Homes," *National Public Radio*, May 12, 2012, www.npr.org/2012/05/ 12/152578740/how-tv-brought-gay-people-into-our-homes.

20   See all of StriveTogether's resources at: www.strivetogether.org/ resources.

21   You can download a template of the spreadsheet at www. livingcities.org/resources/313-data-inventory.

22   "Kresge and California HealthCare Foundation Provide at Least $5M to Organizations That Can Help Health Centers Serve More Patients," http://kresge.org/news/kresge-and-california-health-care-foundation-provide-least-5m-organizations-can-help-health.

23   Explore the data for yourself by visiting the Economic Graph at www.linkedin.com/company/linkedin-economic-graph.

24   Collective Impact Forum, "When and How to Engage the Private Sector in Impact," July 14, 2015, https://collectiveimpactforum.org/blogs/9406/when-and-how-engage-private-sector-collective-impact.

25   Learn more about this guide at https://www.millerheiman-group.com/sales-ready/

26   Read more about the framework in "Nonprofit-Corporate Partnerships: A New Framework," https://ssir.org/articles/entry/nonprofit_corporate_partnerships_a_new_framework

27   You can download an exercise to help you think through your "wedding seating chart" at: www.livingcities.org/resources/298-wedding-seating-chart-exercise.

28   Alison Gold, "What Barriers? Insights from Solving Problems through Cross-Sector Partnerships," *Living Cities*, September 2013.

29   Ibid.

30   Living Cities, "What We Learned About Collective Impact Through Raising the Blended Catalyst Fund," *Living Cities*, www.livingcities.org/blog/1053-what-we-learned-about-collective-impact-through-raising-the-blended-catalyst-fund.

31   Definition from the Global Impact Investing Network, https://thegiin.org/impact-investing/.

32   "How Big Is the Impact Investing Market?" *Global Impact Investing Network*, https://thegiin.org/impact-investing/need-to-know/#s8.

33   Ben Hecht, "#BensTake: Harnessing the Promise of Impact Investing So It Lands in Places," *Living Cities*, www.livingcities.org/blog/789-benstake-harnessing-the-promise-of-impact-investing-so-it-lands-in-places.

34   Ben Schiller, "How Small, Local Businesses Can Reach New Investors and Keep Dollars In Communities," www.fastcoexist.com/3042672/how-small-local-businesses-can-reach-new-investors-and-keep-dollars-in-communities.

35   "From the 4 Cs of Credit to the 4 Ps of Pay for Success," *Living Cities*, www.livingcities.org/blog/798-from-the-4-cs-of-credit-to-the-4-ps-of-pay-for-success.

INDEX

Printed in the USA
CPSIA information can be obtained
at www.ICGtesting.com
JSHW011750051023
49755JS00005B/124